The Essential Guide to
Taking Care of Behaviour

The Essential Guide to Taking Care of Behaviour

second edition

Paul Dix

Longman
is an imprint of

PEARSON

Harlow, England • London • New York • Boston • San Francisco • Toronto • Sydney • Singapore • Hong Kong
Tokyo • Seoul • Taipei • New Delhi • Cape Town • Madrid • Mexico City • Amsterdam • Munich • Paris • Milan

PEARSON EDUCATION LIMITED

Edinburgh Gate
Harlow CM20 2JE
Tel: +44 (0)1279 623623
Fax: +44 (0)1279 431059
Website: www.pearsoned.co.uk

First published as *Taking Care of Behaviour* in Great Britain in 2007
Second edition 2010

© Paul Dix 2007, 2010

The right of Paul Dix to be identified as author of this work has been asserted by him in accordance with the Copyright, Designs and Patents Act 1988.

Pearson Education is not responsible for the content of third party internet sites.

ISBN: 978-1-4082-2554-7

British Library Cataloguing-in-Publication Data
A catalogue record for this book is available from the British Library

Library of Congress Cataloging-in-Publication Data
Dix, Paul.
    The essential guide to taking care of behaviour / Paul Dix. – 2nd ed.
       p. cm.
    Includes bibliographical references and index.
    ISBN 978-1-4082-2554-7 (pbk.)
1. Classroom management. 2. Behaviour modification. I. Title.
    LB3013.D584 2010
    371.39′3–dc22
                                    2010005345

10 9 8 7 6 5 4 3 2 1
14 13 12 11 10

Typeset in 11/14 pt ITC Stone Sans by 3
Printed by Ashford Colour Press Ltd., Gosport

For Ellie, Alfie and Bertie

Contents

Preface

You don't need a personality transplant to learn and apply behaviour management strategies that work. Neither do you need to follow religiously the teachings of the latest 'guru' or sacrifice your teaching style for the latest system. *The Essential Guide to Taking Care of Behaviour* shows teachers how to manage and improve behaviour successfully whilst maintaining trust and positive relationships with students. It encourages you to create the most valuable framework for behaviour management and improvement, one that you have designed to meet your needs and those of your students. It does not advocate a particular 'system' or suggest that there are magic bullets for solving the increasingly complex issues facing teachers every day. Use it as a self-training manual: develop your existing skills, build confidence in your capabilities, design your own resources, create your own realistic action plan, learn flexible strategies and understand why your own behaviour is so important.

The Essential Guide to Taking Care of Behaviour is not just a complete course for managing behaviour; it is a proven method to improve behaviour and the work of teachers and students alike.

Foreword

When you see a good teacher in the classroom or practical area, behaviour management seems effortless. Classes are relaxed and good humoured, the students are attentive and engaged in the learning, relationships are positive and there is mutual trust in the room. Students who are challenging elsewhere seem to have undergone a miraculous transformation. Other staff accept that the teacher has orderly classes but often attribute this to strength of personality, time in the institution or physical presence in the room. The teacher's behaviour management skills are rarely discussed because they are applied so discreetly that they are difficult to identify, let alone emulate.

Yet teachers like this have not woken up one day with the gift of good behaviour management. What are the skills that they have honed over time? What strategies are disguised by the fluency of their teaching? How do they get through an entire lesson without breaking out in a rash brought on by stress?

I spent long hours preparing schemes of work and lesson plans in anticipation of starting my first post. I thought hard about the students I would be teaching and how to engage them in an exciting educational adventure with me at the helm. Armed with lever-arch files stuffed with carefully prepared resources, I skipped to my first class ready to educate and inspire. I was confident, well-prepared and eager to impress. The students, however, had their own agenda. They had been taught by supply teachers for the last two terms and had very different expectations of their new teacher. Within five minutes of starting the class, two had climbed out of the window, one was swinging on the curtains and the others could not be persuaded to interrupt their game of table football, which was by now reaching fever pitch. I called for help and a senior colleague arrived.

Silence and calm descended in an instant. The students listened intently to him, and with coats off and pens out, we were now ready to start the lesson. As he left I thanked him and turned to address the class who, noting his departure, had returned to their former pursuits: a game of coin football waits for no man. Driving home after that first day I was close to tears. I resolved to seek out those teachers who had the skills that I was lacking and learn them – quickly.

It was to those early mentors that I owe so much. Their classes were lovely places to be in: positive, caring and full of good humour and focused learning. They showed me how to:

- communicate my expectations to the students explicitly
- gain a perspective on my emotional state
- empathise with students' individual needs
- remain consistent and fair
- manage confrontation and challenging conversations
- use praise and positive reinforcement instead of constant sanctions
- begin to build relationships with students who presented the full range of challenging behaviours.

Through them I learned that accepting support was not a sign of weakness but a necessary stage in my learning. It also served to demonstrate to the students that I was not alone but part of a strong team working to help them make better choices.

I wondered how long it would take for me to gain the respect that those mentors had. Honestly, it wasn't until the end of the first year that I began teaching some truly effective lessons. It was a tough place to work.

After four years of learning and additional training, I was leading the whole staff in implementing a new behaviour management policy and my entrance into a classroom now had a similar effect as had the senior teacher's on that first day. I had cracked it. It was time to move on to a new post at a larger inner-city school. I approached this new post brimming with confidence; after all, I had behaviour management down to a fine art and had been there and bought the T-shirt years before.

Walking into my first class, full of the skills of an experienced teacher, I could not understand why the students were not listening, why silence had not descended and why the same panic my first ever lesson had elicited was rising inside me. A difficult day turned into a difficult week and a difficult first term. I could not see what had gone wrong. Slowly I realised that these students did not know my rules, my expectations and, most frustratingly, they didn't know that their teacher was one of the good ones. After sifting through my notes and reflections I returned to the strategies that had helped me in the past. Gradually I began to translate the skills I had learnt in the previous school to my new post. A valuable lesson was learnt: regardless of my presumed authority it was vital to concentrate on the basics, the strategies that I knew worked.

About the author

'To punish me for my contempt for authority fate has made me an authority myself.'

(Albert Einstein)

Paul Dix leads a team of behaviour and motivation specialists who are creating unprecedented change in UK schools and colleges. Paul is a leading writer for Pearson/Longman, his courses have been 'Course of the Week' twice in the *Times Educational Supplement* and he is a National Training Awards 2009 winner. Paul is a trainer with an exceptional reputation for designing and delivering training that promotes real change.

Paul trained at Homerton College, Cambridge, and has taught in a wide range of schools and colleges in challenging circumstances. His work was highlighted by HMI and Ofsted as a key element of the work that led to turning round a school in 'Special Measures'.

Paul co-founded Pivotal Education in 2001. As the lead trainer, Paul has been training teachers, head teachers, lecturers, youth workers, advisors, students, mentors, and classroom assistants from early years to adult education. His work on behaviour, motivation and assessment is being used successfully in colleges, schools (mainstream and special), referral units and teacher training programmes in the UK and abroad.

His 'Taking Care of Behaviour' and 'Managing Extreme Behaviour' courses have both been featured as 'Course of the Week' in the *TES Magazine*.

Paul is author of the UK Government's 'New Deal Mentor Training Programme'. His work has been featured on ITV, Teachers' TV, BBC and *The Guardian*. His first book, the *Pivotal Behaviour Management Handbook*, was reviewed in the *TES* as 'Terrific'.

Paul is a behaviour expert for the *TES* and writes for *Teach Primary!* magazine, *The Independent Schools Magazine*, *Didactics World* and *Teaching Expertise* magazine.

You can keep up-to-date with Paul's work on the Pivotal Blog, www.pivotaleducation.com/behaviour/blog.asp.

You can book Paul for training and keynote speaking by emailing ellie@ pivotaleducation.com.

Acknowledgements

There are many people who have contributed to the development of the ideas and thoughts in this second edition. Thanks to the Pivotal training team – Bill Gribble, Alan Davison, Helen Day, Sian Luscombe, Barry Stay, Miller Thompson, Chris Sweeney, Joe May, Chrissie Spring and Ellie Dix – who have taught me so much and bring so much experience.

Publisher's acknowledgements

We are grateful to the following for permission to reproduce copyright material:

Russell Hoban (2002), *Riddley Walker*, London: Bloomsbury.

Every effort has been made by the publisher to obtain permission from the appropriate source to reproduce material which appears in this book. In some instances we may have been unable to trace the owners of the copyright material and would appreciate any information that would enable us to do so.

Using this book to train yourself

The Essential Guide to Taking Care of Behaviour is designed for individual teachers to use and does not rely on institutional change. Whether you are honing, brushing up on or learning new skills it is important that you prepare yourself fully before trying them out with your class. It is easy to learn about a behaviour management strategy that seems sensible, put it into practice quickly and give up after a few days as it doesn't seem to be working. At the end of each chapter you will be asked to commit to strategies for 30 days; to change learned cycles of behaviour and replace old habits.

The book is designed to help you train yourself:

- The chapters are ordered so that you can build your skills and decide on the strategies that you use in manageable steps.
- The training activities are designed to allow you to monitor, develop and reflect on your own practice.
- Decide on your own realistic and carefully time-managed goals.
- The common pitfalls are highlighted and there is advice on how to avoid them.
- Guidance is given on structuring the implementation of new ideas.
- Key strategies and ideas are highlighted for Primary, Secondary, FE and HE.
- The benefits for teachers and students are clarified.
- The website at www.pearsoned.co.uk/essentialguides contains support materials and templates to personalise resources for your classroom.

Allow yourself time to think through, practise and implement the strategies. You may want to focus on one class as a 'pilot' group before introducing the techniques to all of your classes; perhaps start with the class that you currently have least difficulty with.

Don't expect your new skills to work first time or every time. This course is a fast-track introduction to techniques that you will hone over time and throughout your career. With professionalism and diligence the approaches explained in this book will work. They are being used right now in schools and colleges all over the UK, even with the most challenging students.

Creating your own behaviour action plan

As you progress through the book there are opportunities to add to the design and structure of your individual behaviour plan. You will find a printable template on the website where you can input your choice of strategy and plan for implementation. At the end of each chapter there is space to record the main strategies/ideas that you wish to put into action. Although I have suggested some key ideas, you should develop and select those that are most relevant for your classroom, keeping the timescale and number of action points realistic.

As your first step, answer the true/false questions below and add comments to explain your response. It will help clarify your current views on behaviour management and allow you to re-examine your current philosophy. My thoughts and responses to these questions can be found on www.pearsoned.co.uk/essentialguides.

True/False

Parents should teach their children how to behave.   T/F

Boys are generally more disruptive than girls.   T/F

The behaviour of my classes is a reflection of me as a teacher.   T/F

Students from different cultures learn differently.   T/F

How I feel affects the way I teach.   T/F

Children do not need to be thanked for behaving well in class.   T/F

Even good teachers have problems with students.   T/F

Human beings are mainly motivated by reward.   T/F

Consistency is the key to managing behaviour.   **T/F**

It is acceptable to shout at children to get them to behave.   **T/F**

Children who don't attend regularly deserve to fail.   **T/F**

People learn best when they are in a trusting relationship.   **T/F**

Fear is a useful control mechanism in the classroom.   **T/F**

The management of behaviour is different from the management of learning.   **T/F**

Managing behaviour in the classroom

Things to think about before you start

'Don't judge each day by the harvest you reap but by the seeds that you plant.'

(Robert Louis Stevenson)

Lesson planning

I am addressing 'lesson planning' first because it is, without a doubt, critical to the management of behaviour.

The quality of your planning will have a direct effect on the behaviour in your classroom and whilst this handbook can address the management of behaviour it does not seek to do so in isolation. You can learn the latest strategies and techniques, you can have a bulging toolbox of ideas, but sit your students through relentless PowerPoint slides, or give them worksheets, and their behaviour will seem unrepairable.

Give yourself a fair chance to manage and improve behaviour in your classes by planning interesting, exciting and at least engaging lessons. Poor or uninspiring planning will make behaviour management an uphill struggle from the start of the lesson. Do away with worksheets, cloze procedures (fill in the gaps worksheets), word-searches, PowerPoint tedium, copying from the book or board, schemes that you have no ownership of, and any other planning and preparation shortcuts. Your students will know that they are being 'occupied' and will respond accordingly. Instead, be creative in your planning. Plan lessons that engage the students in their learning. Take some risks, small ones at first, and try a more active approach. Get them on their feet and doing as well as in their seats and working. Active learning works. Students really appreciate the change to their routine that an active task gives. Just follow a student around for the day and you will be surprised, and shocked, at just how many lessons follow the 'Sit down, shut up, read the screen and work. I'll be at my desk' approach.

If your planning and preparation of lessons is not immediately appreciated or students respond negatively to lessons that you have spent a great deal of time on, tempting you to say 'I spent hours on those discussion cards and you kick them round the room/rip them/eat them!', don't give up. It takes time to change the expectations and learning habits that students have built up about what should happen in a lesson. As with behaviour management, you have to play the 'long game' and not expect immediate or even short-term gains.

Examine your schemes of work, lesson plans and resources carefully:

- Do they match your students' ability and interests?
- Do they interest or excite you? Is there risk and tension?
- Are they relevant, stimulating, dynamic and differentiated?
- Do they challenge pupils to think in different ways?
- Are lessons planned with timings recorded and pace in mind?
- Have you taken into account different learning preferences and cultures?
- Do your lessons provide opportunities for individual, paired and group work?
- Is there space for autonomous and active learning?
- Do you build in opportunities for self, peer and group assessment?

Prepare lessons that do not rely on you holding the attention of the whole class for more than 10 minutes of a 50-minute lesson. Strictly limit the time you spend talking to the whole class. Time yourself: you may be shocked at just how long you are expecting them to listen actively. In all of my observations, extended 'teacher talk time' is a major cause of disruptive behaviour and restless students. Try to set up activities that enable you to practise your behaviour management strategies with individuals and small groups. Consider preparing instructions for learning activities in written form for the students, so that lessons rely less and less on you addressing the whole class.

Policy and practice

Check your institution's behaviour policy. Some of the decisions on school/college-wide classroom rules, sanctions and rewards may have been made for you and you will be able to dovetail your new learning rituals with these.

Familiarise yourself with the procedure for calling for support from a senior colleague/site security during lesson time. If there is no policy, make a laminated card that explains that you need immediate assistance. When this need arises, you can send the card to the office with a reliable student. You might need to make an arrangement with your head of department/area, head of year/key stage or other appropriate colleague.

Your classroom

Arrange your classroom so that you can get to each student quickly and easily without disturbing or moving others. Think carefully about the classroom configuration that works for different groups. You may have to train students to move the furniture around but it may well be worth the investment of time if less behaviour issues arise.

Designate areas of the classroom specifically for behaviour management displays and make them prominent. The displays are for your use as well as that of the students and you need to be able to read them from anywhere in the room. Make sure that they are not obscured from view by your desk or cupboards and are in large type. The best displays are those which the students have designed and/or created, but you may wish to prepare them in advance. Displays will gently introduce students to the changes that you are going to make and make it easy for you to put new rules, rituals and notices up quickly.

Your classes

Have a seating plan for all new classes and keep it under constant review. Insist on starting with your plan and use it as leverage with students as reward or sanction.

If you haven't yet learned the students' first names give them a badge to wear until you have (younger students can make them). Learn the names as soon as possible. The students will remember yours immediately and addressing students as 'you' or 'red jumper' is not a good start to a productive relationship.

Why not try this?

A quick self-audit of your current practice

Current practice	Always	Sometimes	Rarely	Never
I shout at students				
I worry that I might have been too harsh on a student				
I am consistent in managing behaviour				
I tell students the rules for my classroom				
The hard-working students get forgotten				
I find myself in unpleasant confrontations with students				
I focus on rewarding good behaviour				
I chase up students who miss deadlines and detentions				
I communicate with parents about behaviour issues				
I seek support and advice on dealing with students with challenging behaviour				

Why it is fun to be bad

'I have failed with this boy.'

(Maths report, Paul Dix, aged 15)

The level of academic qualifications that it takes to become a teacher selects out of the profession nearly all of the people who spent their young lives breaking the rules.

Put simply, many teachers do not understand the pleasure of rule breaking, the attraction of dangerous substances, the thrill of criminality or the challenge of taking on authority. As I was one of the few who made it through, perhaps I can shed some light.

There are lots of root causes why students misbehave or fight against authority but there is also challenging behaviour without logical explanation. Students who have come from homes where they are loved and cared for, students who are emotionally secure, able and attend every day, students without medical conditions or mental health problems, still behave inappropriately. Why? Because it is fun! It makes the day more interesting, enhances reputation, provides entertainment for everyone and is an opportunity to challenge adults and authority safely, playing with the lines of tolerance. Breaking the rules has tangible rewards. It brings praise from friends, excitement and danger, increases adrenalin, releases serotonin. It delivers physical and mental pleasure. While some teachers, parents, and large sections of the media consume their time with the search for reason and bemoan the failure of a generation, the vast majority of children who break the rules are doing so because it is fun, an adventure, an exploration of the boundaries of authority and a distraction from the monotony of some lessons.

Some students have good reason to be angry. Others are angry without cause. They use anger as a defence, to test your reaction or as an amusement. They are able to time their anger, switch it on and off and use it to effect maximum disruption to your lessons. It is these students who can often be the most challenging.

I am not discussing this to make you throw in the towel but to encourage you to recognise the primary cause for inappropriate behaviour and begin to use this knowledge. Giving your energy to the search for logic and reason in disruptive behaviour may well be better spent searching for strategies to make it less fun and less rewarding for students.

TOP TIP!

To make rule-breaking less fun:

Clearly define rules, rewards and sanctions and implement them without extreme emotional reactions.

When students are deliberately disrupting your lesson keep your response assertive, controlled and simple: disruption becomes less rewarding.

Keep discussions about behaviour discreet and private whenever possible (one-to-one rather than in front of peer or class group).

Reflect on moments when the student is scoring points; be proactive by predicting these moments and manoeuvering around them.

Don't complain about students publicly or do anything to advertise their status, enhance their reputation or cement their label as a 'troublemaker'.

Try not to reveal or display your 'emotional buttons', e.g., 'Any more of that and I am going to lose my temper', 'You are making me very angry; stop it now.'

By using acknowledgement, praise and reward as the cornerstone of your practice you slowly make it more attractive to follow the rules.

Managing your own behaviour: modelling social and emotional literacy

'I had a terrible education, I attended a school for emotionally disturbed teachers.'

(Woody Allen)

The principle

In order to manage the emotional behaviour of your students you need to provide them with a strong model for appropriate emotional responses. This should be your primary focus as a 'role model' for your students. You need to demonstrate and be explicit about how you, as an example of a successful learner, deal with your own emotional responses and keep them in check. Students need to feel emotionally secure in your classroom to use the rational part of their brain to deal with learning and behaviour challenges. An environment that relies on emotional responses from the teacher to manage behaviour is a difficult and often frightening place in which to learn.

The practice

Teaching is often a performance, yet no one with a heart has to pretend to be pleased when students behave appropriately; it is when the boundaries are crossed that the finest performance must emerge. When Trevor chews the curtains he expects my emotional response. This is precisely what he doesn't get. Breaking this cycle is the key to managing even the most challenging students.

Monitor and check your own behaviour in front of the class. This is particularly important when getting to know a new group of students. They are watching for your reactions and may be testing when emotion takes the place of reason in your reactions; they want to know how to 'push your buttons'. Make a resolution not to shout or show anger as a part of your teaching style. There will certainly be times when you need to raise your voice or shout to prevent a dangerous situation but these should only be exceptions to the rule. When you shout at students (and all humans) they feel threatened and their reflex reaction will be 'fight or flight'. The hypothalamus reacts by sending a signal to the adrenal glands that in turn pump adrenaline into the bloodstream. The emotional brain takes over and the rational part of their brain that we need for higher order thought is temporarily blocked. That is why shouting 'ANSWER THE QUESTION' rarely gets a positive response.

> 'Stressed individuals can't concentrate. In almost every way it can be tested, chronic stress hurts our ability to learn. Specifically stress hurts declarative memory (things you can declare) and executive function (the type of thinking that involves problem solving). Those, of course, are the skills needed to excel in school and business.'
>
> (Dr John Medina, 2008, Brain Rules: 12 Principles for Surviving and Thriving at Work, Home and School)

You can short-cut the management of behaviour with young children. Raising your voice has an immediate effect, threatening tones land with impact and hard stares still have some danger about them. As children grow older some adults get stuck using the same unsophisticated responses to inappropriate behaviour. As hostility begins to lose its impact, rather than change the approach many adults simply try to intensify their response in the hope that it will still have an effect.

The perception becomes that change will happen when the children change. The truth is that to change the behaviour of those around us we must look to what we can control absolutely – our own response.

How we perceive inappropriate behaviour is crucial. Emotions follow thoughts like ducklings following their mother. Think of it as a personal attack, a sign of a society in decline, a symptom of an uncontrollable generation, a product of poor parenting or of 24-hour news media and it is difficult to stop emotion getting in the way. See it for what it really is, a young person testing the boundaries, trying to provoke an adult, trying to relieve the boredom of the day, and it is easier to hold on to your rational understanding of behaviour.

When we pass the students' behaviour through our own emotion, disproportionate outcomes are not uncommon.

Student behaviour + teacher's negative emotion = Disproportionate response

We can find ourselves defining and reinforcing this link on a daily basis. 'You are making me angry', 'I am irritated by your behaviour today', 'If one more person asks to go to the toilet I am going to scream!' and 'I find that swear word particularly offensive and upsetting.' We give our students a route map to our negative emotions. We give the most challenging students precision hand grenades that they can lob in at the most inappropriate moments.

Why not try this?

List the behaviours that irritate you most of all. Do it now, your top five:

1

2

3

4

5

Look carefully at this list. Relate the behaviours to the students who perform them best of all and make a commitment to hide the fact that they irritate you. Do it deliberately the next time you are faced with them and instead map the rational consequence with the student, 'If you choose to keep tapping on the desk the consequence will be ...' Hide the fact that these behaviours that irritate you and in time the students will try to get your attention in less provocative ways.

Model the behaviour that you want to see in your students. Arrive on time for your lessons, prepared for and enthusiastic about learning. Try not to show negative emotional reactions to the class when you are confronting undesirable behaviour but instead explain your frustration as calmly and clearly as possible. You do not need to do this immediately. 'When I walked away from our discussion about the mess on your table I did so because I was feeling cross. I gave myself time to think and work out what to say to you. We now need to have a polite conversation and find a solution to the problem.' Leave your purely emotional reactions for the privacy of home or friends where you are not the role model.

Your students are trying to learn how to deal with their feelings; they need you to model explicitly how you deal with your own. Remember that students may have learned emotional reactions and outbursts from home that are not appropriate for the classroom. I had a student who would persistently shout at me and other students during lessons for no apparent reason. It wasn't until I visited his home to talk to his parents about it that I realised it was not an aggressive response. There was no volume control in his family at all. They all spoke very loudly, all of the time, regardless of the proximity of others. It took a long while for him to find an appropriate 'voice for the classroom' and understand my expectations.

Don't challenge students' prior learning openly but do so by providing a strong model for appropriate behaviour. Save your emotional response to behaviour for when things are going well. Let your students see your enthusiasm for learning, love of teaching and delight in their success. Show them the passion of your positive response. Mark it clearly. When you must intervene with challenging behaviour things need to be very different.

TOP TIP!

Think carefully about how you create a learning environment where all students feel emotionally secure and have the time, opportunity and space to think and speak freely. Examine your most basic routines. When you finish giving instructions for a task add: 'Is there anyone who has any questions about this task? Please ask now if you don't understand as it may be because I haven't explained it properly and that is my fault'. It will encourage students who are still unsure about the task to ask questions without feeling they are at fault. When students have difficulty answering a question in front of the class try, 'Take a moment to calm down and work out what answer you are going to give. I don't mind if it doesn't come out right first time. You know I don't always say things clearly the first time.' Try to make them feel safe enough to take a risk with their answer.

You might prefer to start exploring some of these ideas by focusing on a small group of students rather than the whole class. Let them see you count to ten, take deep breaths, pace the room, relax your thumbs, recite a mantra or whatever method you use to keep your emotions in check. Talk to them about their learning, how they feel when they meet and attempt tasks that are challenging, unfamiliar or new. Then talk to them about your experience of learning. Demonstrate how you work around the frustration of not knowing the solution straight away. Record their responses over a series of lessons and use them as your 'pilot' group. Post the lists on the wall, where they will highlight some key terminology, serve as an aide-mémoir for managing emotional responses and demonstrate that learners of all ages have to find ways through the frustrations of learning.

Strategy spotlight

Give students 'thinking time' to prepare their answers before any hands go up. Try reducing the use of 'hands up', which relies on a few quick thinkers and makes everyone else feel either inadequate or slow. Consider introducing more subtle rituals for attracting the attention of the teacher. I often use, 'Look at me when you have the answer, look away while you are thinking.' Students enjoy the discreet nature of the communication and everyone gets the space to think.

It isn't always easy to check your emotional responses, and at times even the most experienced teacher may be unable to stay calm and controlled. We are not emotionless automatons or tick-box teachers, but as human and fallible as our students. Aim for responding calmly and rationally 8 out of 10 times. If you fall off the wagon don't dwell on your mistake but deal with the fallout in an emotionally mature way. Explaining why you reacted as you did, and apologising if necessary for an extreme emotional reaction, will also be a positive model for the pupils.

As we teach young people that consequences are not personal retribution we begin to erode the 'them and us' culture. The aim is to leave students feeling responsible for their behaviour rather than angry at their teacher. You don't have to have a personality transplant to be effective in managing behaviour. You might, however, want to suppress your natural instinct to react with emotion. You may want to show Trevor that although others may respond to his behaviour with hostility you are playing a different, longer-term game.

By modelling and actively encouraging a calm and consistent approach to learning in the classroom you will start to develop an environment that is free from tension and fear. You will afford students the security and space they need to access higher-order thinking skills and control their own behaviour. Trust will begin to develop.

Watch out for ...

● Making judgements about students because of their emotional reactions. Keep in mind that your students will be at very different stages in their development of emotional control. It is your responsibility to teach them appropriate and proportionate responses, helping ➜

Watch out for ... continued

them to understand why persistent displays of raw emotion can be so disruptive to their learning and the concentration of others.

- Expecting students to have instant empathy with your situation. Explaining that you have just come out of a meeting with the Head, have 35 reports to write by Thursday and have an Ofsted inspection next week means very little to Year 4. It is more useful to explain that you are feeling snowed under by work and share with them how you plan your time when this happens.

Reflecting on practice

Warning – labelling is damaging to you and your students

The inner or private voice that we all use for mapping our own under-standing of the working world must be constructed with positive checkpoints. Labelling damages your relationship with the student, the student's self-perception and your ability to manage your own behaviour. It reinforces the student's negative view of their teacher, perpetuates undesirable cycles of behaviour and leaves your language littered with negatives. If in your head you are thinking, '9C are loonies, book-munching headbangers, if Chantelle Adams is in today it's all over before I open my mouth, they're just losers, how do you teach the little ****s ?', you are unlikely to reach that positive and assertive attitude that you will no doubt need for the next hour or two. Neither will it allow you to examine the strategic changes that need to be made rationally. If you catch yourself using negative labels in the staffroom there are some compelling reasons why you need to check your own behaviour.

The teacher who tries being positive in the classroom only to broadcast negative stereotypes among colleagues will not be able to sustain the separation of attitudes for long. Staffrooms often reinforce unhelpful labels of students/classes/year groups too easily. The joking seems harmless enough at first and relieves the frustrations of a few. But there are dangers lurking. As the jokes are repeated they become common parlance. Groups of staff begin to refer to Year 3 as 'little buggers' and Year 11, Set 5 as 'the benefit squad'. It begins to affect how you view individuals and your expectations of certain classes. It also begins to change how colleagues view you. Just as the students make judgements on your consistency, fairness and integrity, so do your colleagues. What from the inside seems like harmless banter is open to a wide range of unenthusiastic interpretations of your character. Wise profes-sionals stay clear of public and even private verbal attacks on students. When they are confronted by negative labels and stereotypes they seek to challenge them with care, as they would in the classroom.   →

In institutions where there is a high frequency of challenging behaviour the murmurings can too easily combine to become a strong voice. Unfortunately the voice does not look for intelligent solutions but is a defensive response designed to shield teachers from responsibility: 'They are unteachable, what chance have we got with parents like that; what hope is there for these kids?' I have worked in situations where many staff were supremely confident in their ability as teachers, safe in the knowledge that they were not to blame for the appalling behaviour of their classes. Their negativity crossed over into the classroom and students began to get the message that they were uncontrollable. A minority of students leapt on this opportunity to escalate the frequency of extreme behaviour and the balance of power was disturbed. It took months to re-establish the status quo and years to improve the behaviour of teachers and students.

In teaching you have to play the cards that you are dealt. You can spend many years decrying the system or the ills of society, or sticking labels on students to reinforce your own negative map, but it won't help you manage the behaviour and learning of the students sitting in front of you. Neither will it help you to sustain a positive and assertive voice in the classroom. Moreover, students, and particularly those from struggling communities, deserve to have teachers that are unerringly positive, consistent, accountable for their actions and who take responsibility for the behaviour of their classes.

Why not try this?

Find a quiet space to complete the task below. Give yourself 20 minutes to complete it, in silence and without a break.

Continue the passage below. Use the writer's 'rules' for spelling, punctuation and grammar and copy his style so that a reader could not see where the writer stopped and you took over.

lorna said to me, 'You heard the story of why the dog wont show its eyes?'

I said, 'No, I never'.

She said, 'That's what happens with people on the way down form what they ben. The storys go'. She tol me the story then. This is it wrote down the same:

Why the Dog Wont Show Its Eyes

time back way way back befor people got cleaver they had the 1st knowing. They los it when they go the cleverness and now the cleverness is gone

→

as wel. Every thing has a shape and so does the nite only you cant see the shape of note nor you cant think it. If you put your self right you can know it. Not with knowing in your head but with the 1st knowing. Where the number creaper grows on the dead stoans and the groun is sour for 3 days digging the nite stil knows the shape of itself tho we don't. Some times the nite is the shape of a ear only it anint a ear we know the shape of. Lissening back for all the souns whatre gone from us. The hummering of the dead towns and the voyces befor the towns ben there. Befor the iron ben and fire ben only littl. Lissening for whats coming as wel.

Time back way way back 1 time it wer Ful of the

(The extract is reproduced from Russell Hoban's *Riddley Walker*, 2002, Bloomsbury)

_____

_____

_____

_____

_____

_____

_____

_____

_____

_____

_____

_____

_____

_____

_____

_____

This task was originally used by Malcolm Reed from Bristol University PGCE English Course.

After completing the task, fill in your personal reflections opposite.

Personal reflections on the task

My emotional reactions to the task:

My rational response to the task:

Students who have a reading age lower than that of the resources you provide have similar, if not stronger emotional responses. A student who has a reading age more than two years lower than their age (not at all uncommon) will experience these frustrations throughout the day and in most of their classes. Clearly no one can comfortably live with the constant challenges this creates. Students, as adults, find ways to protect themselves. They may become withdrawn and avoid work discreetly or, at the opposite end of the scale, engage in a range of more disruptive work-avoidance techniques.

When I give this task to teachers on training courses the same reactions are displayed. Those who are highly literate and emotionally secure enter into the challenge with enthusiasm. Others seek support from people sitting close by, make paper aeroplanes with the sheet, repeatedly complain about the task and, in one memorable incident, became so angry and frustrated that he stood up in front of 250 others, holding the paper and shouting, 'This is SHIT'. These reactions are typical of teachers who are successful learners; university educated, academically inclined and experienced professionals.

Keep this in mind when applying the strategies in this handbook and setting expectations for behaviour. My question to teachers is always, 'If these are your reactions to challenging learning situations what should we realistically expect of the students we are challenging?'

Key ideas summary

Key idea	Benefit for the teacher	Benefit for the students
Model the behaviour you expect from students.	You will develop a heightened perspective on your own behaviour as you focus on what your audience are seeing and hearing.	Students see clear models of appropriate behaviour for a learning space.
Explain to students what techniques you use to keep your emotional responses in check.	Being explicit about your own behaviour allows you to deconstruct reactions to emotional responses, examining cause and effect.	Students become aware of a variety of techniques to stop the emotional brain hijacking the rational brain and with support will develop their own techniques.
Design your learning environment and routines to provide emotional security for students.	There are fewer emotional flashpoints in the lesson; the classroom is a calmer place in which to work.	Students who were previously reluctant to speak out find their own voices.
Create some checklists and charts that map how to deal with emotional outbursts or mounting frustration. Display them and use them with the students.	The display is an aide-mémoir for the teacher to use when frustrations begin to take over.	Students have a visual map of steps they can take to adjust and manage their own behaviour. Anger is defined and rationalised.

Practical strategies for Primary, Secondary, FE and HE

Primary

Don't relate their behaviour to your emotion. Change 'Do you realise how that behaviour makes *me* feel?', to 'Can you imagine how your behaviour affects other people?' Even better, relate the behaviour directly to the student's choices and leave the connection between behaviour and consequence free from emotion.

Agree a set of three symbols that students can use to indicate how they are progressing with the work. As they are working they place one fact at a time on the desk: a smiley face for 'I'm doing well and don't need help', a straight face for 'I need to ask a question but I am getting on' and a worried face for

'I need help'. Make sliders with the children from bookmarks or flags to place on the desks for group work.

Secondary

Beware of issuing sanctions with emotion. The more frustrated we feel the more likely we are to go for the most severe consequence straight away, 'Right, I am going to have you excommunicated, banned, imprisoned and flogged!' The behaviour rarely warrants such a severe sanction, it is our emotion that ratchets it up. When you feel the emotion surge, delay the decision with, 'I need to think about what you have just done' or, 'I am sorry that you are having a bad day, take a moment to calm down and we will talk about what happens next.'

FE and HE

Students may come from schools where they are used to being shouted at. When they come to college they want to be treated like adults and are old enough to realise that the emotional response is a loss of control. Convince them that they have entered the adult world by refusing to shout in anger. You risk reminding them of behaviours that you really want them to have left behind. Your emotional patience is crucial in showing them that things have changed.

Introduce subtle mechanisms for students to give you feedback on your teaching and their learning. Ask them to grade the homework so that you know how useful they found it, invite anonymous written evaluations or ask them to grade your teaching. Your honesty about your own fallibility and willingness to accept the view of others is a strong model.

30 days to make a change

Think about the changes that you would like to make in how you manage your own behaviour. This might relate to an individual student, class or context. Commit to the new strategies for 30 days to allow them to embed into practice and your own teaching style.

In 30 days I will walk into work and ....

....

....

....

....

Make a commitment to try some of the strategies that have been suggested in this chapter.

My personal resolutions are:

1 _____   Review date _____

2 _____   Review date _____

3 _____   Review date _____

Establishing and sustaining consistency and certainty

'When one admits that nothing is certain one must, I think, also add that some things are more nearly certain than others.'

(Bertrand Russell)

The principle

Being consistent in dealing with the behaviour of your students means that they know what will happen if they choose to break the rules, and equally they know what will happen if they choose to follow the rules. They view you as fair and predictable. When they walk through the door into your classroom they know what to expect there. Moreover, they are certain that their behaviour has a direct effect on your responses.

Your consistent and well-managed classroom environment is a safe and predictable place in which to learn.

The practice

It is not easy to be consistent and it often requires a great deal of emotional control. Inconsistency, at best, results in your students being wary of you and, at worst, leads to resentment and confrontation. Becoming agitated by the fifth latecomer who interrupts the lesson and sending them outside the moment they open the door, relieves your tension briefly but sends confusing messages to the rest of the class. Inconsistency with your students can also result in your weekends being peppered with regret and worry that you have misjudged a situation or student.

'Fairness' is very important in classrooms. Persistent inconsistencies in your behaviour can damage relationships. It is hard work trying to remain consistent and fair all of the time. Consistency does not simply emerge, consistency needs a plan.

Strategy spotlight

When you next reflect on an incident and decide that your actions were not consistent:

● Meet the student when you both have time to talk

● Apologise for your inconsistency

● Explain that your goal is to be fair and consistent and you will be open about mistakes

● Thank the student for being patient with you

● Record the development of the relationship from this point onwards.

Make it clear to students that they should talk to you, in private, if they feel that they have been treated unfairly. Model an appropriate way of complaining for the students: be explicit with tone and language. Let them know when the best time to approach you would be; you may find it useful to display a procedure for grievances on the wall. This will not stop all students complaining defensively when faced with high-level sanctions, but you will be surprised by the students who do use the system and give you pause for thought. You may need to demonstrate carefully to students how to accept an inconsistent action/sanction/comment without reacting immediately. Once they are sure that the complaints procedure works, they will have more confidence in doing this. When students use the agreed system you should listen with care and see it as an opportunity to reflect on your own practice and build relationships. Be prepared for and encourage other students to support those who find it difficult to approach you directly.

When you hear students talking about their teachers they discuss those who are consistent ('Don't mess about in her lesson, she always gets you') and those who are not ('I hate him, he send me out for nothing, I only asked a question' (sic)). They also recognise those teachers who use praise more than sanctions ('She never shouts, she's really nice, I can just get on with my work'). They know when you are late to the lesson, unprepared, impatient or react with more emotion than thought. They are forming opinions about your consistency that are quickly set and hard to change. Students bring these attitudes and expectations to your classroom and begin the class with them. Lessons can feel like an uphill struggle when students expect to be treated unfairly or lack a consistent model. The more they sense inconsistency the more they will be tempted to exploit it or work against it and the classroom becomes an unstable place for learning.

Reflecting on practice

I remember being unfairly harsh on a Year 11 class who met me for the first time and were still grieving over the loss of their previous teacher. It was a difficult lesson, fuelled by emotional energy on both sides and I was inconsistent, unfair and angry. I left the lesson worried that I had blown it. I reflected that I could not ignore my own behaviour when I met them again and needed to address it with them.

I opened the following lesson by apologising for my behaviour and being as honest as I could about how I felt. They listened intently and without comment. The mood in the room eased and the lesson was calmer and more productive. The foundations for our relationship had been set. Later in the year the same class commented that they had been shocked by my willingness to apologise and that their worries about me had been diffused. If you reflect on your interactions and decide you have been inconsistent, find time to apologise to the students.

In order for your students to be clear about which consequences (positive and negative) follow certain actions, you need to display your responses to explicit behaviour clearly. The more consistent you are with applying these consequences, the more the students will become 'certain' that poor choices will result in sanctions and good choices in rewards. When discussing behaviour with students talk in terms of 'certainty' – 'If you stay on task throughout my lessons you can be certain that I will acknowledge it and give you praise and reward. If you choose to break the rules you can be certain that you will receive sanctions that I will enforce.'

This can take some time so you need to be dogged in your persistence. If you place a heavy focus on praise and rewards, you will have a better chance of success and the pace of change will be accelerated. Rely on sanctions and your behaviour management may be effective in the short term but you are storing up problems for the future. Without a balance between sanctions and praise/reward there is little motivation for students to make better choices – 'He is in detention with me every week but it doesn't seem to make any difference to his behaviour.'

| Reflecting on practice |

Inconsistent (or just differentiated)

The fact that you use your professional judgement to reinforce positively the behaviour of some students more than others does not make you inconsistent. Some students need to hear your acknowledgement and verbal praise more often than others. Their short concentration span or low self-belief needs the gentle nudge of your encouragement to keep them working. Others appreciate recognition of their good choices every now and then. However, many students receive very little acknowledgement and praise and can easily be forgotten, particularly when there is a heavy focus on disruptive students. It would not be fair to heap material rewards on challenging students simply because they decide to follow the rules: your thanks and/or praise is sufficient.

You are differentiating your responses according to the needs of your students just as you differentiate your lesson content. It is this differentiation that needs to be consistent for the individual. Try not to get caught up worrying about how you can be consistent across a year group, or even across the whole school, instead focus on individual classes and, whenever possible, on how you are being consistent with individual pupils.

With sanctions the situation is somewhat different and you need to be consistent in their application across the class. It is important that students know that each member of the class has the same sanction applied using the same tariff. If they sense unfairness in this area it will damage your relationship with them. The only exception to this is when an agreement has been made with a particularly disruptive student, and this will usually mean that the sanctions are harsher or applied with more rigour than those that apply to the rest of the class. You are unlikely to find the rest of the class complaining too much about this and they will already be aware that the student in question has different needs from theirs.

Be comfortable with differentiating strategies for individuals or classes: this does not make you inconsistent.

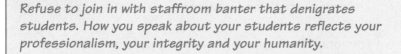

TOP TIP!

Refuse to join in with staffroom banter that denigrates students. How you speak about your students reflects your professionalism, your integrity and your humanity.

I have worked in schools where the heavy focus on sanctions was not balanced with strategies for positive reinforcement, praise and reward. The sanctions were well supported by all levels of management and class teachers were able to place students in detention whenever they felt behaviour was inappropriate. These detentions, held twice weekly, were vigorously supported by the management team and in the first few weeks of the new system there had been some measurable improvements in behaviour around the site. Intrigued by the effect of this punitive system I asked to look at the statistics for numbers of students in detention. On the week that I visited there were 236 students in detention out of a school of just under 1000. Class teachers were delegating responsibility for following up incidents to the management team and although behaviour around the site had improved (perhaps due to their fear of the senior staff who held all the power), behaviour in classrooms was beginning to slide. The system was nearing collapse as students grew resentful of frequent, high-level sanctions and the deputy head struggled to keep up with all of those who owed multiple detentions. Balancing the system with graduated rewards and reconnecting class teachers with their responsibility to deliver graduated sanctions reduced the number of detentions significantly. It left the senior teachers with more time to prioritise those students who needed most support.

Consistency in practice

- Consistent **language**; consistent response: What are the messages that could be reinforced through agreed use of certain cues?
- Consistent **follow up**: Ensuring 'certainty' at the classroom, faculty and senior management level.
- Consistent **positive reinforcement**: Routine procedures for reinforcing, encouraging and celebrating appropriate behaviour.
- Consistent **consequences**: Defined, agreed and applied.
- Consistent, simple **rules/agreements/expectations** referencing promoting appropriate behaviour.
- Consistent **respect from the adults**: Even in the face of disrespectful students!

- Consistent **models of emotional control**: SEAL (Social and Emotional Aspects of Learning) that are modelled and not just taught.
- Consistently reinforced **rituals and routines**: In classrooms, around the site, at reception, etc.
- Consistent **environment**: Display the quality of a good primary school, consistent visual messages and echoes of core values, positive images of students rather than marketing slogans.

Your consistency is not only judged by the students but also by other staff. If you need to call on support from colleagues they need to be sure that you have followed the agreed procedures in spirit and in deed.

As an 'on call' teacher, discussing behaviour with a student who has been thrown out of the lesson for a minor misdemeanor is not easy:

'Ok, tell me what happened.'

'I got sent out.'

'You must have done something.'

'No, really, he just threw me out without a warning and I was only chewing gum.'

'Err ... right.'

When colleagues begin to hear feedback regularly from students about your inconsistency their support naturally wavers. Dealing with minor indiscretions with high-level sanctions without warning is just 'crying wolf': when you really need support it may not be there. Demonstrating your consistency to colleagues as well as students means that you can be trusted implicitly. When the time comes that you need to rely on the vocal support of colleagues (and it will) and/or the support of the students you can be sure that it will arrive in force.

Watch out for ...

- Judging yourself too harshly. We need to be consistent but we are not mechanoids. There are days when we feel shaky, tired, irritated and just want to run for the nearest beach. Days when Colin's persistent whispering seems designed as a slow torture. Days when, despite our best efforts, we deliver an unfair consequence or act that is out of character. Don't beat yourself up over these occasional lapses. Remember that you are the adult, the professional, and it is your responsibility to control the urge to throttle. Take a step back and use the techniques that work.
- Worrying about giving out too many rewards and/or sanctions. At first the students will test the system. You may find yourself flooded →

Watch out for ... continued

by requests for rewards and/or spending a great deal of time giving and chasing up sanctions. Expect this stage in the introduction of new boundaries (positive and negative). When the students feel the system has been sufficiently tested and they can predict your responses accurately, things will level out. It is not unusual for groups of students to reach the most serious sanctions repeatedly in the first few weeks. Do not be put off by this, stay consistent and students' choices will change.

Reflecting on practice

'No trainers means no trainers' – enforcing a rule

The strongest team and the one that can have most impact is the whole staff team. When staff in extreme circumstances have unity of purpose and keep to agreed procedures they can effect significant change.

Students at Community School X would wear trainers to school as a matter of course. It was by no means the worst example of breaking a rule in the school, but enforcing it was a key step in restoring the balance of power in an increasingly tense environment. The original rule of 'black or brown formal shoes' had been worn down over many years. This was partly because students were so persistent in their desire to wear trainers, partly because teachers had grown tired of confronting students, and partly because parents, trying to keep up with the price of trainers, did not have enough money to buy two pairs of shoes. Mobilising the whole staff into pushing the issue to the top of their radar, using a rigid procedure supported at all levels of management and communicating clearly with parents solved the problem. All parents were written to and given notice that the rule would be strictly applied after the summer break. The procedure for students with trainers was simple: parents would be contacted, the students would be sent home to change and as a last resort they would be kept out of lessons until school shoes appeared. Only a medical note would excuse a student in trainers and even then these would need to be black.

As a staff body we would confront any student wearing trainers, and extra checks were put in place at key points – leaving PE/Drama, leaving the last lesson of the day, end of morning and lunch break. At the start of the new term there were 50 students who arrived in trainers, a week later it was 28 and within a month there were no students out of school uniform. A

→

27

great deal of work had been put in by all concerned. Nobody looked forward to those difficult conversations with parents ('Yes, but I can't afford to buy him another pair of shoes') or to isolating students from their classes but the effect was indisputable. The process and the product served to prove a much-needed point for the staff: it was possible to effect significant change in student behaviour. We began looking for other things that we wanted to change.

Why not try this?

List the most frequent positive and negative types of behaviour students exhibit in your classroom in the table below.

Positive behaviour	Negative behaviour

Decide on three rules that will operate in your classroom. They should be ones that cover as many of the above examples of behaviour as possible. If you know that you can efficiently negotiate the rules with the class, then do so. Otherwise you may want to wait until you have developed stronger relationships before you negotiate anything. For now you are the teacher; it is your classroom and if you want to, you get to decide what the rules are.

If you use the learning rituals as described in the next chapter then 'Follow the learning ritual' might be your first rule. In time you may want all activities to fall within these rituals, but to start with you may find it useful to choose **two or three** further rules. Phrase the rule so that you are reminding students of the behaviour that you want to see rather than constantly reinforcing the behaviours that you don't want. The aim is to start telling them on, rather than telling them off.

Which rules would be most important in your classroom?

- When someone is talking, listen, or, one voice only
- Stay 'on task'

- Bring the correct equipment (including homework) to the lesson
- Try not to disturb others who are working
- Stay in your working area
- Follow instructions first time, fast
- Listen, commit, engage
- Phones, music players and electronic equipment must be turned off and kept out of sight
- Speak politely to staff and students
- Follow the teacher's instructions straight away.

Rules

1

2

3

I find frameworks for applying rules, rewards and sanctions that use graduated sanctions easier to work with. One alternative to this is a points system where all students begin with, say, 20 points each. Tariffs are matched with different challenging behaviour and staff remove points from a student's total. My experience with these models is that they can:

- encourage confrontation when applying sanctions as you are taking something away from the student, so their focus on rewards can easily be lost
- create an opportunity for a student to lose all of their 'chances' in one day
- be more open to abuse by angry teachers: 'Right, that's another 5 points off.'

With a graduated rewards-and-sanctions framework there are no points and everyone starts with a clean sheet every lesson. Students can clearly see what the consequences of their actions will be and can make decisions accordingly.

Decide what sanctions will appear on your graduated list for students who choose not to follow the rules. You should make it clear to students that if there is a serious incident, such as violent or dangerous behaviour or verbal abuse directed at the teacher, you will not use warnings or other graduated sanctions but take immediate steps to remove the student or call for support.

→

You can choose to have one or two verbal warnings before more serious sanctions are applied. Be explicit with your language when phrasing your rules. Avoid loaded phrases such as 'respect' or 'manners'. Use the 'Popular sanctions' lists on page 32–35 for ideas. Each time a rule is broken the severity of the sanction should increase.

Now work out an appropriate scale of rewards. Again there is a list of ideas below to get you started. Rewards should be desirable, age-appropriate and easily organised. You may choose to have different rewards lists for different classes.

Display this chart on the walls of your teaching space and explain it to the students. Use and keep to the rewards and sanctions you have listed. Don't deviate from the plan. When you catch students following the rules, reward them; when you see them breaking the rules, warn them and then deliver sanctions. At the end of the first week review the chart and explain any changes to the students. Be prepared for students to challenge rules, rewards or sanctions that don't appear on the chart; they will help to keep your responses consistent.

Graduated sanctions

1st	Verbal warning
2nd	
3rd	
4th	
5th	
6th	

Graduated rewards

1st	Verbal praise
2nd	
3rd	
4th	
5th	
6th	

Popular rewards

(Remember: It's not what you give, but the way that you give it that counts.)

Private/discreet verbal praise

When you sincerely communicate to students how pleased you are with them it builds trust in the relationship and motivates them to sustain their efforts. It is the most important reward that you can give to your students (see Chapter 6).

Post-it praise

Subtly sticking a Post-it note on the desk of a student who deserves praise is discreet written communication that disturbs no one.

Your time

Students need to know that they can get your attention by fair means rather than foul. Reinforce this by giving students your time in extra study groups and individual support as part of your rewards.

Positive notes home

The most desirable reward for many students is positive communication with parents.

Type up and photocopy sheets of A5 or A6 with:

*'Dear Parent/Guardian, Just a quick note to say how pleased I am with ....
......'s work/behaviour/commitment in class today. If you would like to follow up with a reward at home it would be well deserved.'*

Keep a stack on your desk and use them as a higher-order reward. Students will value these notes more than you might imagine. I taught a girl who still used one I gave her in Year 8 to wave at her parents when they questioned her school/social life balance. (See www.pearsoned.co.uk/essentialguides for printable examples.)

Positive phone call home

This is the one reward that seems least appealing for the teacher at the end of the day yet is the most direct pathway you have to building a partnership with home. If you don't know the parents well, keep it quick and simple. Plan what you are going to say and how you are going to end the conversation. I use 'Hello, it's Mr Dix, Keenan's English teacher, I've got some good news, do you have a moment to talk?' and, to end, 'I am sure you don't want to spend your evening on the phone to me, thank you for your time.'

Homework pass/extension

This is a token given and signed by the teacher to allow the student permission not to do the homework or hand it in late as appropriate.

Positive referral

Send a student, either during the lesson or at an appropriate time, to see a colleague for further acknowledgement and praise.

Merits/stickers/star charts/stamps

If your school does not already have a policy, or has one that is solely related to learning, you need to create a cumulative rewards system with tangible rewards at, say, 15, 50 and 100 points to support good choices in behaviour. Record merits in students' individual exercise books or homework diaries. Use an ink stamp or sheets of stickers or bits of paper with your signature and keep a record yourself.

'Leave first' token

Reward students who have worked consistently well with a token they can cash in when they want to be first out of the door. Very useful if you have the students before break, lunch or at the end of the day.

Subject/class award certificate

Use as a higher-order reward and send a copy direct to the parents/guardians.

Choosing where to sit

Earning the right to negotiate over their place on the seating plan.

Popular sanctions

Warnings

One of the most frequent complaints from students who are removed from the room is that they didn't realise they had been given a warning. Find a way of clearly marking the moment that you give a warning: take the student aside, place a note on the desk, make a note on the register, or, for younger students, place a name on the board. You can then refer the student to that moment later on.

Impositions

Students are given additional work to do at home that, when completed, is signed by their parent/guardian. Type up the instructions for the task and have five or six different ones photocopied so that you have them ready. Make a note at the bottom of the imposition explaining the consequence of not handing in the work before school the following day. The work should be linked to their work in class, relevant, appropriate and differentiated to take half an hour of the student's time. Do not give lines or repetitive tasks as these are completed with resentment rather than thought.

Reparation

A structured meeting with the student where choices are discussed, boundaries reconfirmed, undertakings given and, most importantly, the relationship between the teacher and the student protected. This should take no longer than 15 minutes and must be held with the class teacher. In many institutions this has been introduced in place of traditional detention systems. The change in emphasis has had a profound impact on teacher–student relationships and significantly reduced the number of students receiving after-school sanctions. (See 'Detention v Reparation' in Chapter 10.)

Lunchtime detention

I have never been keen on detention as a sanction unless I have an opportunity to discuss the students' choices with them during it. After-school detentions are difficult to enforce, cause complications with the timings of families and eat into students' life out of school. Lunchtime detentions are easier to enforce and have more effect. Keep the detention to 15 minutes; the length of detention will not determine whether the student chooses to repeat the behaviour; it is your conversation that has most chance of making an impact. Use the 15 minutes to reinforce and renegotiate expectations, perhaps find an opportunity to build your professional relationship with the student.

A moment after class

Hold the student back after class very briefly to discuss their poor choices. You are showing them that you care about the choices they make in your lesson. This is appropriate for students of all ages and adult learners.

Class report

Keep a brief record of the student's behaviour in each lesson over an agreed period. Explain that when it is complete a copy will be sent to the parents, Deputy Head, etc. At the end of each lesson read the comment to the student and ask them to co-sign the report. Be prepared to reward better choices. In individual lessons apply your rules and rituals to students on report in the same way as others.

Time out

Give time outside the classroom, ideally supervised by another colleague, to allow the student a few minutes to calm down and rejoin the lesson. The language is important here. A 'time out' is less aggressive than being 'sent out' and echoes 'time out' in sport where players are given time to calm down away from the field of play.

Phone call home

An effective sanction but one that must be handled with care. Take advice from a senior colleague about the home situation and likely impact of the call; many parents use corporal punishment and this association may not be desirable. Think carefully about the time that you call and prepare what you are going to say and how you are going to end the conversation.

Moving a student (to sit elsewhere in the room)

It is important that when a student reaches this sanction it is delivered privately, preferably away from other students. If the interaction is too public you risk involving others and causing humiliation.

'Parking'

Gentler terminology for moving the student out of the classroom to sit with or 'be parked' with another teacher who is teaching another class. Make prior arrangements with a senior colleague so you can send the student with his or her work. Give the student a prepared note or laminated card to take. Have a look at your school policy as it may determine what happens to students who have to be removed from the lesson.

Key ideas summary

Key idea	Benefit for the teacher	Benefit for the students
Apologise to students privately when you are inconsistent and unfair.	You are building positive relationships with your students. Your honest self-reflection is the mark of an effective professional.	They see you as fallible and human. Students are given a clear model for how to apologise for mistakes.
Have a procedure for students to complain if they feel they have been treated unfairly.	Challenges to your decisions are not public and are brought at an appropriate time and place.	Students have a mechanism for complaining that is structured and mirrors those in working environments.
Design and display a list of graduated rewards and sanctions.	As well as providing a useful reminder while you are teaching, the lists give structure even when frustration begins to creep in.	Students know what will happen if they choose to break or follow the rules.
In the first instance it is your responsibility to decide on the rules, rewards and sanctions that operate in your classroom.	You are able to spend more time teaching and less time negotiating.	Students know that the teacher is in control of the framework for behaviour management, in particular that rules are not negotiable.
Show consistent behaviour to your students by arriving at lessons on time, well prepared and with enthusiasm for learning.	Your modelling of appropriate behaviour and organisation for learning space will positively influence your students. Your timekeeping and preparation give you a platform from which to monitor others.	Students have a clear model to use and interpret. They are enthused by your energy and given a clear example of appropriate self-discipline and personal organisation necessary for successful learning.
Start with a blank sheet for every lesson.	Your expectation of a student in a single lesson is not coloured by previous incidents. All students have the chance to make good choices.	Students have the opportunity to change their behaviour. They know that you will always judge their behaviour fairly and in context.
Have a clear system for calling on support from colleagues when critical incidents occur.	There is a mechanism for dealing immediately with violent/abusive/dangerous behaviour.	Students know that there are some behaviours that require immediate referral and high-level sanctions.

Strategies for Primary, Secondary, FE and HE

Primary

Post your rules/rewards and consequences using words and symbols. Consider using photographs of students to place alongside them which demonstrate the behaviours that you want to see. This is useful for children with autism and Asperger's as they have a clear visual model of the desired behaviours.

Use cues to indicate quickly which stage of the sanctions/rewards children have reached. You might code S1 for sanction number 1. 'I have given you a warning, I know that you would rather not move to S2, let's see how I can help you with this next question.' Or quickly in the to and fro of a busy classroom, 'Darius, you have chosen S3, you know what to do.' Try traffic lights, steps on a ladder or Nuclear emergency states: 'Chelsea, we are now at Defcon 4!'

Secondary

Use class rewards. Post a sheet of A4 paper on the wall with a tally chart entitled 'Class reward'. Any student can earn a class reward point and once earned they cannot be taken away. Once the class reaches 20/40/60 points the class earns a reward. Differentiate the target total to keep your classes motivated; the class that struggles to begin the lesson will need a shorter-term target than the one you can already get working. Make the rewards age-appropriate and desirable. For instance they might be able to listen to music while they work, work outside in the summer, have extended story time. You may choose to negotiate these rewards in time and ask them what they think appropriate rewards (that don't involve money!) might be.

Use positive notes and use them regularly. Consider setting yourself a target to give out 10 every week. Students love positive notes because they can use them at home to get positive reinforcement and rewards. They also like them because it will make the people at home proud – but don't expect them to admit to that! So many schools have positive notes printed which languish in a filing cabinet in the admin office or in a box under the Head of Faculty's desk. Place them on your desk, waft them gently as you walk around the classroom and make them a central part of your rewards strategy.

FE and HE

Spend time creating display that reinforces your consistently high expectations of the students. This might be a traditional display of excellent work, a map that shows the educational routes taken by you and your fellow lecturers, or a working display that collates thoughts, ideas and questions. When I talk to teachers in FE about displays in a primary school they look wistful and give a contented smile. Many then list the reasons why they couldn't replicate this at the college. Those who create teaching rooms packed with displays create a stimulating, owned and consistent learning environment.

Take time to agree the boundaries for your classroom or practical area. Post up the boundaries with 'Staff and students have agreed to ...'. Make sure that you personally adhere to the rules and model this to the students, 'I am turning my phone off and putting it in my bag, I would be grateful if you did the same now, thank you.' There is nothing that erodes boundaries quicker than the teacher who gets caught texting under the desk.

30 days to make a change

Think about the changes that you would like to make in your consistency and certainty. This might relate to an individual student, class or context. Commit to the new strategies for 30 days to allow them to embed into practice and your own teaching style.

In 30 days I will walk into work and ....

....

....

....

....

Make a commitment to try some of the strategies that have been suggested in this chapter.

My personal resolutions are:

1 _____   Review date _____
2 _____   Review date _____
3 _____   Review date _____

Learning rituals, rules and routines

'Habit is something you can do without thinking, which is why most of us have so many of them.'

(Frank A. Clark)

The principle

Students need to have your expectations for learning clearly explained and posted on the walls of the classroom. It is not enough to assume or expect that students know how to behave. To manage and improve behaviour you need to teach it. Rituals are short lists of rules for behaviour and/or learning targeted at a specific activity or at specific behaviours. Do not expect your students to guess the rules for each activity in the classroom as they will not be the same as those of other teachers. When the rules for each type of activity (e.g., sitting on the carpet and listening, working in groups, quiet individual study, going outside to play, entering the classroom, not wielding the scissors) are clear to everyone, students can then choose to follow these rules and receive acknowledgement, praise/rewards, or not to follow them and receive a warning(s) followed by sanctions.

The practice

Do not assume that students know how to behave in the classroom. Regardless of their age, teach all of your students the precise rules for each task. Good Early-Years teaching is a strong model here as teachers of this age group spend a great deal of time initiating and negotiating learning and social rituals. From working in groups to moving furniture, from entering the classroom to asking for help, there should be clear rituals that everyone understands how to follow. Some of the rituals will be simple, such as indicating to the teacher that you need help by turning the cup on your desk upside down; some more complex and structured, such as steps in negotiating group roles.

Break down each different learning ritual into what is expected at each stage. Spend time teaching this. For more complex rituals, involve them in creating attractive displays in the room on large chart paper, memorising the steps or chanting the ritual as a class. For simpler rituals, use modelling and rehearsing, reinforcing appropriate use of the rituals with positive reinforcement. Phrase your rules positively: avoid use of 'do not' and 'no'; avoid absolutes such as 'silence' and value-loaded phrases such as 'polite' or 'respect'. At each stage describe the desired behaviour, e.g., 'When someone is speaking, listen' or, 'Look at me.'

Teach the new rituals immediately before the task, giving examples and modelling your responses carefully. When the task is revisited it is vital that you run over the routine with the students. When the activity begins, focus on those students who are following the rules of the learning ritual and use praise and positive reinforcement to support their good choices: 'Thank you, this table; you have stopped your conversations, got your pens out and are listening. That is number two on our agreement: well done.'

When students choose to break the rules, give a clear, private, verbal warning. 'You have chosen not to follow the third part of our learning ritual. You have chosen to receive a verbal warning. I need you to follow the agreed plan. I will come back in a while and will be looking to praise better choices.' If the rule is broken again, apply the next sanction on your graduated list. Indicate, by taking the student over to the display, which rule has been kept/broken to reinforce the ritual. Introduce only one new ritual at a time and teach it until the students know it without looking at the display and begin saying 'Alright, enough, we know the routine!'

As a new teacher taking over a class you can make good use of routines and rituals that have been established with the students by colleagues. This serves two purposes: it connects the routines in your room with those of an established member of staff and ensures that students are familiar with the routines, meaning that you don't need to reinvent the wheel. Investigate the existing rituals that the students understand and know from other teachers and use them when appropriate, e.g., students who study Drama may have been taught advanced rituals for devising performances in groups. These rituals can be utilised in many subjects but particularly English, PSHE, History and RE.

Reflecting on practice

A colleague fed up with students ignoring signs demanding that they put their phones away decided on a different tack. On top of a filing cabinet in the corner of the room she placed a fish tank with old mobile phones and music players gently floating. On the first day of a new course the students would walk in, immediately notice the fish tank and urgently enquire what purpose it served. 'Oh,' she responded casually, 'those are just from students who decided to take their gadgets out in my lesson last year.' Stunned, the students would immediately secure their own devices and not risk taking them out. Now I am not suggesting that you should be actually confiscating equipment and putting it in water, but it is a light-hearted way to make an impact with a sign and certainly was noticed far more frequently than a 1980s mobile phone with a red cross through it.

In work with schools and colleges I have further developed the idea of more engaging signage to focus on different rituals and rules for different areas of the site: signs woven into the carpet tiles, signs and procedures taped to the floor of the canteen, images projected onto white walls in the entrance hall, 3D shapes and hanging mobiles with rituals written on, and touch-screen flashbooks to engage students with and remind them of the agreements. Developing the wording to be more gentle, inclusive and respectful also helps students to understand rather than rebel against these rituals and rules.

Examples of school/college signage:

You are now entering a learning area.

Thank you for turning your phones off.

It's a respect thing! Or:

- Follow directions
- One voice at a time
- Demonstrate respect for students and staff
- Enjoy your learning and helping others to learn
- Arrive ready to engage in the learning.

Or:

Everyone has the right to work in a safe, productive environment.

Expect to be challenged if your conduct falls below our agreed standard.

And certainly <u>not</u>:

Rules for the Learning Resource Centre

No mobile phones

No eating

No drinking

No music players

No loud talking

No shouting

No online games

No petting!

TOP TIP!

To help you to manage low-level disruption:

*Set private, manageable short-term targets for individuals.
Adjust the seating plan in time for the next lesson.*

Re-establish the routine, then catch students who are following it.

Tackle behaviour patterns as soon as they begin.

Look for an opportunity to help, 'Show me how I can help you'.

> Re-examine your positioning in the room.
>
> Continue using non-verbal cues.
>
> Use 'I understand …', 'I hear …', 'Maybe it is …' to return students back to work.
>
> State your request and then walk away and give the student take-up time.
>
> Drastically reduce time spent talking to the whole class.

Tackling persistent latecomers

Institute or agree a clear ritual for all students who choose to arrive after the lesson has begun. Post the routine on the door. 'If you arrive after the lesson has begun these are the agreed steps …' To discourage lateness consider placing a chair by the door with a 'sign-in' sheet, students who arrive late sit in the chair and wait until you are ready to speak to them or ready to invite them to join the class. You may decide that students who arrive late lose their choice over where they sit or that they must speak to you for one minute after the lesson. A gentle, ritualised deterrent in this situation is as effective as heavy sanctions. The information that you collate on the sign-in sheet is useful evidence if you are to really hold up the mirror to the student and show them the evidence of their behaviour. It is also invaluable as data to present to parents.

Now start gently, but persistently, going out of your way to improve your relationship with the student. Say hello to them and smile when you pass the student in the corridor or at the school gates. Be persistently good humoured even when your greeting is rejected or ignored. Persist with this for three weeks. Every day. Acknowledge the student, exploit shared interests and invest some of your time building trust. Your professional relationship with the student is your greatest lever. Build a positive relationship and you can nurture a genuine motivation for the student to be punctual.

Finally, randomly reward the students who have arrive on time while swapping some of the most exciting parts of your lesson to the beginning from time to time.

Persist with any new strategies for at least 30 days. Through clear expectations, improved relationships and a small measure of cunning the student may be able to resist taking the long way round to your classroom.

Watch out for ...

- Displaying the rules, but discreetly and/or in only one area of the classroom. Think about where your rituals are best displayed. A checklist of rules for entering and leaving the classroom should be on the door of the room. Similarly, the rules for individual work at tables need to be visible to everyone as they work.

- Enthusiastically introducing rituals and then not referring to them again until sanctions need to be applied. Use the rituals to support your discussions with students. Point to and refer to them tirelessly until the students realise that you are not going to be diverted from them.

- Establishing too many new rituals too soon. Introduce new rituals gradually and over time. Allow one or two to become embedded in the learning before developing more advanced rituals, such as moving furniture around or class discussion. Too many new rituals too soon are confusing for both teacher and students.

Reflecting on practice

As an NQT covering a foundation class for PE, I was a little nervous. I had heard stories about the 'wall of death' but no one would explain what it meant and there was general merriment in the staffroom as they anticipated my adventure with the 'little people'. I had worked with this age group before but only within classrooms and then only in small groups on very structured tasks. Now there were 35 of them in a huge space and I knew nothing of their normal routines or expectations.

After a lengthy and not altogether calm or efficient 'getting changed' session, 'Just wear your pants then', etc., we walked towards the hall. I could feel the excitement building and they were keen to get inside. I slipped into my usual routine that I would use with Year 5 of leading them into the room and sitting in a circle in the centre. As I walked in, the class began running en masse round and round the hall. I reached for my whistle and giving a loud blast signalled them to stop. Unfortunately they did not recognise this as a signal to stop running and fall silent but returned the sound with whoops and shouts and by running even faster. I realised that I was encircled by the 'wall of death'. The class had clearly assumed that PE was just 'running about' and were having a great time.

I was saved only by a passing colleague (who may have been at the door for some time!) who got immediate results by calling 'freeze', which was a ritual that they knew. He quickly introduced an alligator swamp, lily pads and tunnels into the circuit and together we introduced more rituals cued by single words 'sleep' (for lying on the floor and resting), 'slow' →

(for slow motion) and used pieces of string on the floor to show spaces for small groups to work together. It taught me a great deal about behaviour and classroom management, ideas that I carried forward for older students.

Why not try this?

Create a ritual for entering the classroom and list five observable behaviours that you wish to see from all students. Here are the rules for writing the learning ritual or indeed drafting any student/teacher conduct agreement:

- Ensure the behaviours that you want are identified and encouraged. Students are guided in how to behave rather than in how not to
- 'Don't' and 'No' have little positive effect on behaviour
- If you want clear boundaries, make them simple and precise
- The message should be gentle but persuasive
- The reader must not feel attacked, e.g., 'If students continue to block the toilets we will lock them up'
- Students are involved in the drafting and wording of the agreement.

Have a go at drafting the simplest ritual – entering the room:

Learning ritual for entering the room

1 ....

2 ....

3 ....

4 ....

5 ....

Now re-edit and take out the 'No's' and 'Don'ts' and re-jig them with 'Please' and 'Thank you for'.

Integrating latecomers into the lesson can be very disruptive and time-consuming. Using a ritual for latecomers will not stop all students arriving late but it will help them to check their behaviour and help you to control their arrival so that it causes least disturbance to the class.

What do you want students who arrive late to do? Wait outside and knock? Take the seat nearest the door? See you at the end of the lesson? Wait for an opportunity to join in with the lesson? Go to their seat and get their equipment ready for the lesson? Speak to you immediately on arrival? Sign a late register? Walk in quietly without speaking to other students?   →

Ritual for arriving late

1 ....

2 ....

3 ....

4 ....

5 ....

Post the two rituals on the outside of the door to your classroom so they can be clearly seen by all classes as they arrive at your lesson. Teach the class these rituals step by step, modelling the desired behaviours. Encourage their use with positive reinforcement and praise in the first instance and sanctions when necessary. When the class know these well, think about other rituals that you would like students to use and understand: moving around the room, leaving the room, group discussion, peer assessment.

Learning ritual for peer assessment

● 3:1 positive to constructive criticism: find three things that are praiseworthy in order to earn the right to criticise

● Justify at least three examples by comparing with the exemplar materials

● Agree three written targets for redrafting.

Teach three routines every term and by the end of the year your students will know precisely how they are expected to behave. The more persistent you are the closer to your expectation they will get: 'In this room we do it like this.'

Key ideas summary

Key idea	Benefit for the teacher	Benefit for the students
Use as your starting point the idea that all of your students need to know the explicit behaviours that you want to see in your classroom.	The teacher can decide on the precise behaviours they want to see for each activity.	Students learn the specific desired behaviours that are expected; they are able to make informed choices about their behaviour.
Use language that is phrased positively when drafting your rituals.	There is an implicit expectation that all students will behave and respond positively.	Students begin to hear more positive language being used; their expectations are adjusted accordingly.

Language, performance and positive manipulation

'Language is a map through which humans construct their view of the world.'

(James Britton, Language and Learning)

The principle

Tell a child that he is 'naughty', 'a trouble maker', 'difficult' or 'challenging' and he will include it in his map to understanding the world. Tell him often enough and he will route everything through it. Through careful use of language you can raise self-esteem and help students to make better choices in their behaviour.

The language you use can help to diffuse potential problems in the classroom, protect and enhance students' views of themselves and

depersonalise challenges to their actions. The vocabulary that you use with the students is more controlled when it has been thought through and planned. Relying on improvisation is unreliable and inconsistent.

The practice

As a teacher you are often performing. You may not feel confident, assertive or positive on a Monday morning but you strive to give your students this impression. Perceived weaknesses in your use of language and tone of voice often lead to instructions being ignored or rejected immediately: '*Please* take your coat off, I am too tired to deal with you today', or 'If you are not going to listen to me I cannot teach you.' Making careful choices in your use of language, maintaining a consistent tone of voice and confident intonation means that you can communicate assertively even in a weakened emotional state. This takes some discipline and self-awareness on your part. You need to maintain an assertive performance even when you become weary of the constant interruptions and your emotional brain tempts you into pleading with the students or throwing your hands up and slumping into your chair.

PMS – Professional Manipulative Skill

Manipulation is not a dirty word! It is at the heart of successful behaviour management. Gentle, positive and kind, but still manipulation. Guiding children towards appropriate behaviour and using your craft to discourage argument is PMS (professional manipulative skill).

As children grow older and realise what you are doing the manipulation becomes more subtle. At times it can be laced with the expectation of reward. While most younger children will accept 'Mrs Williams needs your help' without question, a similar request to a worldly Year 5 is treated with some suspicion, 'So you want me to go where? To see who? For what? And you will give me what? Mmm, can I get back to you on that one?'

Positive manipulation is more immediately effective with the majority of children – those who expect to find themselves following the rules. It is the children who come to you with low self-image and an expectation that they will cross the lines of acceptable behaviour where your manipulative craft is really tested. Disconnecting their behaviour with your emotion is a useful first step. Behaviour should remain disconnected from identity to ensure that your message is not confused. 'I like you, I don't like your behaviour today' makes it clear to students that there are appropriate and inappropriate behaviours and not appropriate and inappropriate people. Tell a child that he is naughty often enough and he will believe it. Tell a child he is clever/kind/helpful/thoughtful and in time he will believe in himself.

With children who have a limiting self-belief your relentless pursuit of their positive attributes can make the difference between an okay day and pandemonium. 'Wait, wait, where are my stickers? I can feel this is going to be an excellent lesson.' Your certainty chips away at their negative assumptions and inappropriate habits. Used deliberately, day after day with hard to reach children you can interrupt the negative internal monologue that others have allowed to develop.

Choice

'Choice' is an important concept in behaviour management. When students know the rules, rituals and expectations explicitly, then they can make a choice whether to follow them or not. All human beings make choices about their behaviour throughout the day. As a teacher you are trying to teach students to take responsibility to make better choices about their behaviour. Using the 'choice':

● allows you to attack the behaviour and not the student's character
● puts the responsibility for behaviour onto the student
● encourages dialogue that stays focused on behaviour
● focuses attention on the student's choices and separates them from the behaviour of others
● depersonalises the interaction: 'This is not a personal attack, you have chosen not to follow the rules and I am applying the appropriate sanction.'

Discuss a student's 'poor choices' and 'good choices' in his behaviour, e.g., 'You made some poor choices in your behaviour today, particularly the standing on the chair and throwing your pen down. In tomorrow's lesson I need you to make better choices. I remember last week when you helped me to clear up, that was a good choice.' Help students to learn that all choices have consequences. Present 'closed' choices to students such as, 'You can continue listening to your iPod and then have it confiscated, or you can put it away and carry on with your work. Make a good choice.'

If students want to argue about sanctions or discuss rewards, explain that you will not discuss them in 'learning time' but can find time outside the lesson to do so. You may then have more time to provide more detailed questioning to help the student understand his own choices. For example, 'What do you think the poor choices were that caught my attention?' and 'What do you think you could do to avoid this happening in the next lesson?'

Closed requests

Many teachers, particularly Primary, report the success of prefacing requests with 'Thank you': 'Thank you for putting your bag on the hook', or 'Thank you for dropping your gum in the bin.'

The trust in the student that this statement implies, combined with the clarity of the expectation, often results in immediate action without protest. It is almost a closed request which leaves no 'hook' to hold on to and argue with.

A similar technique can be applied to requests for students to meet deadlines or attend meetings that they would rather ignore: salesmen would call it an 'assumed close'.

> 'When you come today get as close to 3.30 as you can so we can resolve this quickly and both get home in good time.'

> 'When you hand in your coursework next Monday, meet me by the staffroom so that I can store it securely.'

You are assuming and encouraging a positive response, making it awkward for the student to respond negatively.

Why not try this?

Try out the following phrases and linguistic structures to turn a negative response into a positive one. The language has been adapted from sales techniques. You may just find that some work for your style and your students. Enjoy bypassing difficult arguments and skilfully turning a situation to your favour.

1st 'No'

'I am certainly not expecting you to respond immediately …'

'All I am asking for the time being is …'

'Knowing what I know and being as close to the situation as I am I need to tell you that …'

2nd 'No'

'I am not asking you to make a decision now'

'Based on this conversation I believe what you are saying is …'

'Remember this is simply …'

'All I am asking for is 5% of your trust and confidence, I will earn the other 95% ...' (cheesy, but it works!)

3rd 'No'

'There is a very good reason that I have the persistence that I do ...'

'Look what I stand to lose ...'

'Give me your confidence in some small way now and I will ...'

'I don't normally do this but ...'

'I will promise you three things ...'

As a final attempt at getting a positive response try:

'You don't make quick decisions and that is good; I don't make quick decisions either ...'

'Listen, when I am in a situation like this ...'

I am not suggesting that you change your classroom style into that of a used-car salesman. You shouldn't need a sheepskin coat to use the odd technique to sell an unwelcome demand successfully.

Assertiveness

Many teachers recognise that their pattern of behaviour is to be nice or compliant for far longer than they really want until they reach the point of no longer being able to hold it in; then they explode nastily and inappropriately all over students who happen to be around. This can leave students with the impression that there are only two states or behaviours their teacher can do – Nice or Nasty. The shades in between, which is where assertiveness lies, are unused and eventually lost from the repertoire of behaviour management strategies.

Assertiveness is not simply standing your ground, just saying 'no' and repeating your demand (the 'broken record' technique). Just as students have choices so you have the opportunity to choose your behaviour. You have many options as to how you respond to inappropriate behaviour, all of which can be assertive actions. You might choose to record it and address it at a more appropriate time, ignore it, confront it, walk away and consider your response, etc. Assertiveness is knowing that you can control your own behaviour and making considered appropriate choices in your response to students. Don't be afraid of saying 'no' and saying it with impact when it is appropriate. Be careful not to overuse it as it will soon lose its power and damage the atmosphere in the classroom. You risk being ignored if your repertoire of verbal responses is so predictable.

Examples of assertive terminology

'You need to' – speak to me at the end of the lesson

'I need to see' – you following the ritual

'I expect' – a focused ten minutes of work to end the lesson

'I know you will' – look at the learning ritual before starting this task

'Thank you for' – picking the wrapper up

'I have heard what you said, now you must ...' (redirecting the conversation)

'We will' – emphasising shared responsibility

All students, but especially those who have had a string of supply teachers or an unreliable home life, need to hear that you 'care' about them, their work and behaviour. As a class teacher I often told students that 'I'm here for the long term, I care about your behaviour and am going to work with you to help you succeed.' When you apply a sanction it can be softened by explaining that you 'care about his success too much to allow poor choices to stop his learning'.

TOP TIP!

'You don't look like the kind of person who would take a phone out in class' is a more intelligent approach than 'Why oh why have you got your phone out again?' In more tense situations it is this assumption of good character that can help guide children away from inappropriate behaviour: 'Clive, you have made some poor choices today (cutting Sarah's hair being just one of them), I know that you can be very helpful at tidying up, if I give you these books I am sure you will put them neatly on the shelf.'

When searching for an assertive tone it is useful to separate interactions between those that use a 'formal register' and 'informal register'. Your formal register will be used when addressing the class or large groups, when calling the register, establishing routines, dealing with confrontation and disagreement and applying sanctions. If you are carefully considering your choice of verbal language, yet not being heard, it is likely that this register needs most attention.

For a formal register try:

Using a controlled, respectful, but flat voice.

Keeping the pitch of your voice within a 'normal' range. High-pitched voices signal frustration, perhaps signaling a loss of control, while low pitch may signal tiredness or lack of care.

Lowering volume.

Breathing steadily but not audibly!

Maintaining a regular and steady pace of speech.

Your informal register, which you might use when discussing work individually or with a small group, delivering personal praise, talking about areas of shared interest, or welcoming students to the classroom, is equally important but doesn't need too much shaping. Your informal register should be audibly different from the formal: more relaxed, more interesting and varied in tone, pace and volume – the sort of register that you would use with friends and colleagues. Students value being spoken to in an informal register, but not all the time. The balance between the two is critical. Those teachers that have the two registers firmly embedded with students are able to switch from focused work to moments of relaxation/calm/humour and back to hard work. They can choose when they will accept informality and when they must insist on formality. Their students' own language registers are more defined because the model is imitated.

Reflecting on practice

What actors can teach us about shouting

Good actors know that showing the extreme edges of their range is not good technique. What engages the audience is the tension and power that lies below the shouting: once the actor has shown his full anger there is no room for the audience to speculate. The performance becomes more predictable, the character less interesting. Anthony Hopkins' performance as Hannibal Lecter is a strong example of this. There are clear parallels with the classroom (in vocal control rather than Chianti-sipping cannibalism!).

The teacher who shows the limits of his or her range has nowhere to go next. Teachers who repeatedly scream and shout are often ignored. The 'audience' has become tired of the performance: it is expected, predictably irritating and uninteresting.

10 reasons to stop shouting

1   Students resent being shouted at. They see it as an abuse of power.

2   Students see shouty teachers as teachers who lack control. They are either frightened by it or find it hilarious.

3   You would never shout at a student in front of their parents.

4   If your model of behaviour is poor it will affect the way your students choose to deal with each other.

5   Over-emotional responses to inappropriate behaviour will frighten many. It will also encourage others to push your buttons.

6   Your relationship with the student is damaged by shouting; mutual trust demands a more equitable relationship.

7   Colleagues hear your voice echoing down the corridor and begin to question your ability to manage behaviour.

8   Shouting in the workplace is not acceptable behaviour, and so it goes too in schools/colleges.

9   Managing behaviour through fear is unsophisticated and unsustainable.

10 Disproportionate responses to inappropriate behaviour encourage unfair punishment: 'Right, that's it, you are in detention … FOR EVER!'

Whilst our choices in verbal language are important, your voice and physical language also need attention. You can say all of the right things but unless you pay attention to what you are saying non-verbally your point will have little impact.

From the moment you enter the classroom your physical language is read (and misread), interpreted (and misinterpreted) and responded to by students. Being aware enough of your own body language to communicate consistently assertive messages is a very useful skill. It will take time to achieve. As a first step check that you are modelling appropriate body language for a learning space.

At all costs avoid:

Pointing at students with your finger, or at the door, 'Get out!', etc.

Rolling your eyes.

Turning your back on students who are talking to you.

Standing over students.

Invading their personal space too quickly and without invitation.

Demanding sustained eye contact (an aggressive act in many cultures).

Using any form of aggressive touch or gesture.

Dismissive hand gestures.

Trying to confiscate items by snatching them.

Aggressive tensing of the facial muscles, particularly eyebrows.

Using your size to dominate an interaction physically.

Making fast, surprising or sudden movements.

Instead:

Use your whole hand to gesticulate in preference to a pointy finger (or keep your hands by your side).

Show questioning and open faces.

Step back from a difficult conversation to regroup.

Adopt confident and deliberate movement around the classroom.

Use a slow approach to a student's working space.

Hold conversations at eye level with some eye contact.

Maintain a relaxed stance, arms by your side, hands unclenched.

While it is relatively easy to plan to use certain linguistic frameworks, words, registers and body language, it is more of a challenge to monitor effectiveness. In observed lessons ask colleagues to comment on your use of verbal and physical language. Give them a checklist of verbal and non-verbal strategies that you are trying to employ and ask them to observe and give feedback on:

overused words and phrases

students' reactions and responses for changes in language

tone, volume, pace and pitch.

Watch out for ...

● Slipping back into the terminology that you have always used when lessons become stressful and your emotional brain takes over. Practise using new vocabulary and phrases while you are on your way to work so that they become a natural part of the language you are modelling.

● Sending mixed messages to students by contrasting verbal and physical language, e.g., smiling when applying sanctions or giving a reward without establishing gentle eye contact.

● Using open answer questions to tempt your students into negative responses, as in the figure overleaf.

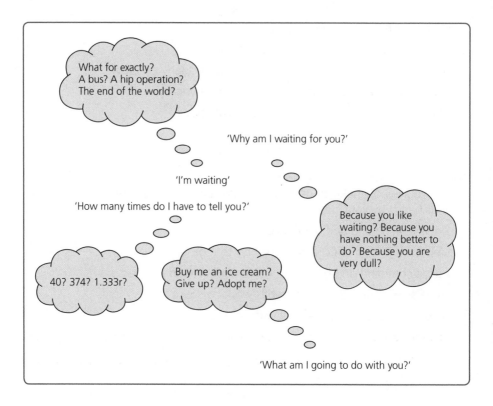

Reflecting on Practice

Silence!

It may be terribly unfashionable but I like to teach students how to work in silence. For many students there is no silence at home or around school and once they experience silence it can be highly addictive.

There was rarely silence in classrooms in Forest School: those teachers who could attain it did so by terror and the majority had given up trying some time ago. As a Key Stage 3 coordinator I instigated silent reading for Years 7, 8 and 9 tutor periods twice a week. There was general disbelief from students but I had a team of teachers who were willing to give it high enough priority. We decided that it was essential that all the form tutors read at the same time and modelled the behaviour they expected from the students. This was backed up with a 'learning ritual' for silent reading which reminded students of their individual responsibilities and a tightening of sanctions for those

→

students who chose not to follow the rules. I supported staff by offering a referral system which would require persistent offenders to read with me and an opportunity for students who read in silence to take the books home. We were fortunate to be able to spend some money and hand-pick books appropriate for age and interest, including graphic novels, fiction and non-fiction.

We worked hard for two weeks: coaching students, following up sanctions, modelling like crazy (to the amusement of the students I would insist they held the book correctly to protect the spine), rewarding students who followed the rules and making it clear to everyone that disturbing the class reading also meant disturbing the teacher. After two weeks something changed. Students started enjoying the silence and the opportunity to read a book; they understood that there was no way of opting out and liked the fact that everyone, including the tutors, was reading. Teachers and visitors passing by silent classrooms with 35 students reading were shocked and impressed. Whole areas of the school fell silent after lunch and it was not long before the scheme was extended to Years 10 and 11. The longer-term benefit on the culture of reading in the school and community and the school results at SATs and GCSE was marked.

Students will remain silent if they know their compliance is for a limited time, purposeful and planned. If you repeatedly and unexpectedly demand silence for long periods without explanation, you are digging a teacher-sized hole to fall into. If you want to ask for quiet, teach the class a ritual, use the countdown technique explained in Chapter 4 or use the assertive instruction 'Eyes on me', or 'I need you to look at me and listen'; explain why you need silence and for how long: 'I need you to stop what you are doing and get your eyes on me for one minute; what I am going to say will help everyone with this task.'

Why not try this?

Complete the exercise comparing the language that you have grown up with, the language you have used in the past and the language you could use now. Start introducing the new vocabulary this week, so that by the end of the week you have weeded out the vocabulary that is not supporting your students' good behaviour. Think carefully about where the language that you have always used has come from – your own teachers, parents, colleagues – and question it hard.

→

What did you say?

Incident – Throwing a piece of paper across the room

What might your teachers have said to you?

'_____'

What would you usually say to a student?

'_____'

And now?

'_____'

Incident – Shouting out in class

What might your teachers have said to you?

'_____'

What would you usually say to a student?

'_____'

And now?

'_____'

Incident – Refusing to follow instructions

What might your teachers have said to you?

'_____'

What would you usually say to a student?

'_____'

And now?

'_____'

Key ideas summary

Key idea	Benefit for the teacher	Benefit for the students
The verbal and physical language used in the classroom is the result of careful planning rather than repeated spontaneous improvisation.	You make conscious choices over the vocabulary and linguistic structures used. When you are under pressure your verbal and physical language remains consistent.	The teacher's verbal and physical responses are predictable. The classroom environment has less tension and is a safer place in which to learn.
The teacher's verbal and physical language is assertive.	The teacher is more likely to get their needs met and correct behaviour quickly and efficiently.	Students are in no doubt about who is in control of the management of behaviour. They can easily understand your instructions and read your physical language.
Discuss behaviour in terms of 'choices', confronting the behaviour rather than attacking the child's character.	The teacher is able to 'depersonalise' conversations about behaviour and reduce the likelihood of confrontation.	Students understand that they are responsible for the choices they make. They soon realise that the sanctions that result from inappropriate behaviour do not constitute a personal attack.
Clearly differentiate between formal and informal language, modelling its appropriate use.	The teacher is able to establish formal and informal rituals in the classroom.	Students learn from and imitate the model, understanding that different situations dictate different forms of language.
Demonstrate and define appropriate physical language for the classroom.	The teacher establishes clear expectations for movement, touch, personal space, etc.	Students feel safe and have a clear model of appropriate behaviour for the classroom.
Steer clear of stock phrases and clichés that have little impact on behaviour.	The teacher is encouraged to create language that is tailored to meet the needs of her students.	Students have less opportunity to undermine the teacher publicly.

Strategies for Primary, Secondary, FE and HE

Primary

With children who are skilled at arguing back and whose arguments flow with such ease it can be hard to get a word in edgeways. A quick 'Thank you for listening' as they pause to draw breath can knock them off course for a few moments so that you can get your message across and withdraw with your dignity intact. Similarly with children who openly break the rules and anticipate the conversation that you are going to initiate, throwing a 'curve ball' can give you the early advantage. Our opening lines are usually the same. The child who is scratching his name on the desk expects, 'Why are you scratching your name on the desk?' He is ready for the interaction, he may have had the same conversation many times. Opening with 'Did you see the hamster running under your legs?' may just give you enough space to correct the behaviour ('No, neither did I but I did see you drawing on the desk ...'), while the child is left ambushed by your diversion.

Secondary

Using phrases that refocus the responsibility for inappropriate behaviour on the students help to keep everyone's emotion in check. I really like, 'I am sorry that you are having a bad day'. It is empathetic without being passive, direct without being threatening.

Most of us have the experience of working one to one with a child and finding ourselves answering questions that in hindsight they ought to have tackled themselves. Filling in gaps in their understanding feels like a useful shortcut at the time, but it can encourage an unhealthy reliance on the teacher to solve problems rather than provide support. Finding the balance is difficult, particularly if your new 'friend' thinks that all the answers have just sat down beside him. If you find yourself drifting into a dynamic where you have become the one answering questions for the student, it is time to pedal the other way.

The skills that you need are commonly found in what is now called 'coaching' (previously referred to as good teaching!). Make a point of countering relentless questioning by reflecting rather than giving advice. You are consciously developing the conversation away from the one about the learning.

'My chart is rubbish, do it for me'	'What could you do to improve this first bit?'
'What do I put here ...?'	'Can you show me what you think ...?'

'Tell me the answer'	'I may need your help to get that far. Can you compare …?'
'Why do I have to do this?'	'Are you able to describe …?'
'I'm bored/tired/suffering executive stress, can you do it for me?	'What would happen if you put your ideas alongside mine …?'
'I don't understand any of this'	'Can you show me an instance when …?'
'Can you read it for me?'	'Perhaps you can tell me the word that you recognise …?'

What you are doing is encouraging metacognitive skills with and for the children. It is these skills which will, in time, help them to successfully manage the frustrations of learning for themselves and overcome them. At first you will need to provide the prompts, in time they will begin metacognitive questioning and rituals in their own heads. The art of the teacher is to know when to hold up the mirror, when to signpost and when to provide the cushions for the softest landings.

FE and HE

Through use of collective language you can make it clear to the students that the expectations are the same for all students and teachers. 'We have all agreed …', 'Our learning contract is …'

If students come to you with a very negative view of their own ability it will have taken years to form. Their language, littered with negative reflections, must be gently and persistently countered. Try:

'What is stupid is that you think you are stupid!'

'Where did you learn that finding something hard means that you are stupid?'

'How does finding fractions hard cause you to be stupid?

'So far you are doing well in Chemistry, soon you will understand this part of the course as well.'

'Pretend for a moment that …'

'Rate your understanding of this on a 1–10 scale.'

'I know that you can't do it yet …'

'Stop and imagine that you could do it easily.'

30 days to make a change

Think about the changes that you would like to make in how you use language. This might relate to an individual student, class or context. Commit to the new strategies for 30 days to allow them to embed into practice and your own teaching style.

In 30 days I will walk into work and ....

....

....

....

Make a commitment to try some of the strategies that have been suggested in this chapter.

My personal resolutions are:

1 _____   Review date _____

2 _____   Review date _____

3 _____   Review date _____

Motivating students: meaningful praise and reward

'People don't care how much you know until they know how much you care.'

(Anon)

The principle

Human beings are motivated by acknowledgement of their work, positive reinforcement, praise and reward. In the classroom, positive reinforcement is the most powerful tool you have for managing and motivating your students. It is also the fastest way to demonstrate to your students that you care. If you positively reinforce the behaviour that you want and expect, students will respond by seeking your attention through fair means rather than foul.

The practice

Praise changes relationships, raises self-esteem, increases motivation and improves attitudes to teacher, subject and school.

Whatever 'carrot' you choose it is not a true reward but a token that represents something far more important. Material rewards offer brief pleasure but not lasting satisfaction. The rewards that students value above others are relational, friendliness, warmth, acceptance, recognition, encouragement, the good opinion of their peers, teachers and parents, gentle smiles of appreciation, a quiet word for some, public praise for others. These rewards are the foundation for an inspirational relationship with a teacher that offers satisfaction today, tomorrow and for a lifetime. Our surveys of students in FE reveal that even most older students cite positive feedback to their parents or a trusted mentor as the most desirable reward.

You need to be intelligent with your use of praise as it has differing effects on individuals. Not all human beings want public praise; in fact many find it as distressing as public admonishment. Hold up work as an example to the rest of the class and a broad smile may open up on the face of one student, but for another it is humiliating, unwelcome and may discourage him from aiming for similar standards in the future.

Acknowledge students who are following your instructions and rituals with a 'thank you' or non-verbal sign (thumbs up, nod of the head) coupled with eye contact. This is a positive reinforcement of their behaviour, good manners and an important step to creating a positive culture in the classroom. I cannot imagine training a roomful of adults without saying thank you; the same follows for students. The better your relationship with the student the more meaningful and effective the reinforcement will be. Many students will be entirely satisfied with regular, sincere positive reinforcement and verbal praise. Their reward is your pleasure and the sense of pride you are helping to nurture.

> ## TOP TIP!
>
>
>
> *Your smiling face at the door of the room is a simple yet highly effective motivator. In a moment you can counter the deflating effects of the commute, the arguments over cereal and inevitable conflicts of busy mornings, 'No, you cannot bring the television to school, etc.' A smile, kind word, perhaps a hand shake does more than just make your students feel happy, it gives them energy for the lesson and a consistent model to look up to. Remind your children*
>
> →

that they are valued and welcome. Convince them that you have been waiting all weekend to see them again! Let them know how excited you are by the plans for today and infect them with your passion for learning. Teachers who sit behind desks and laptops, allow children to drift in on their own and issue the inevitable 'starter is on the board' command, find it difficult to motivate themselves let alone the class.

Students appreciate praise when it is delivered discreetly, privately and fairly. They know that your praise is sincere and deserved. They need praise that is individualised, you need to be prepared to deliver this using your own language and style; repeating 'praise phrases' will not convince anyone that you truly appreciate their work and ability to stay within the rules. Get down to a student's eye level by crouching next to his working table or pulling up a chair. Try positioning yourself so the student has to look down to you (difficult for foundation teachers, I know), it has a very calming effect on the interaction. Try asking the student what they think you are so pleased about, why you are about to give them a sticker/stamp/smile/high grade. By asking them to reflect on their own achievement you are making the praise meaningful to them. In the same way giving your praise a context proves its value: 'That would not look out of place in a professional exhibition', 'That is the most intelligent question I have heard from all of my classes this week.' Teachers working with students who have low self-esteem use reflective and contextual praise as a matter of course. They know that it is vital that the student knows why they are being praised. It chips away at low self-esteem. Wallpaper praise, 'Great, lovely', Personal praise, 'You are brilliant', and Directed praise, 'Great, you have followed our agreed routine', are not remembered by the students. It reinforces so fleetingly as not to be of much value. The reinforcement that students take home with them must be marked by a reflection and/or a context.

'I wish someone had told me that how I felt as a child is how I would feel as an adult.'

(June Brown – Dot Cotton in *Eastenders*)

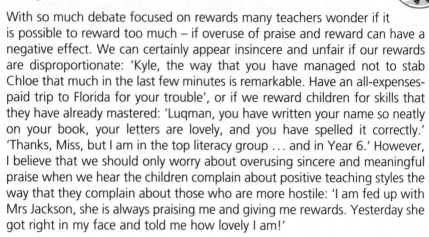

Reflecting on practice

Can you overfeed students on carrots?

With so much debate focused on rewards many teachers wonder if it is possible to reward too much – if overuse of praise and reward can have a negative effect. We can certainly appear insincere and unfair if our rewards are disproportionate: 'Kyle, the way that you have managed not to stab Chloe that much in the last few minutes is remarkable. Have an all-expenses-paid trip to Florida for your trouble', or if we reward children for skills that they have already mastered: 'Luqman, you have written your name so neatly on your book, your letters are lovely, and you have spelled it correctly.' 'Thanks, Miss, but I am in the top literacy group ... and in Year 6.' However, I believe that we should only worry about overusing sincere and meaningful praise when we hear the children complain about positive teaching styles the way that they complain about those who are more hostile: 'I am fed up with Mrs Jackson, she is always praising me and giving me rewards. Yesterday she got right in my face and told me how lovely I am!'

There is much debate about the amount of verbal praise that is appropriate to use with students. Teachers are often concerned that if they use praise too much it will become devalued and they risk highlighting efforts that they see as being 'normal'. There is also a worry that some students will miss out on the praise so it is better kept for special occasions. Their caution often hides a discomfort with using praise and positive reinforcement as part of their teaching style. I think there is some fear lurking also; perhaps the fear of appearing soft, too open, even weak. Yet for the students praise is very welcome; they view you as assertive, interested in their work and at worst a little overenthusiastic. In 20 years of working in schools and colleges I have never heard a student complain that a teacher praises too much. However, I often hear concerns that teachers ignore the efforts of students who work hard throughout each lesson.

Teachers who succeed with students who present high-level challenging behaviours or with early-years students will tell you that they use high levels of praise and positive reinforcement. It is not that they think these children deserve more praise than others, it is because quite simply they know that it works. They are not worried about overusing praise as they know that it continues to have an impact and is a far better behaviour-management tool than sanctions. Students with low self-esteem, poor emotional control or attention disorders need more intensive and regular positive feedback.

Don't reserve your acknowledgement and praise for only the best-behaved students. Reinforce the behaviour of those students who quietly get on with their work, those who find progress difficult and those whose concentration drifts. Differentiate your praise: the student who struggles with written work yet completes the opening paragraph may deserve equal praise to the literate student presenting a finished story. Change your own perspective to 'catch someone doing the right thing'. The accomplished Year 1 teacher who brings her class to order by focusing on the students who are following the rules is a strong example here, 'Just look at Samuel: he is sitting up straight with his table tidy ready to leave for lunch. Well done, Samuel: you can go first.' The same technique with age-appropriate language works for 8 year olds and 18 year olds, 'Thank you this table, you have done exactly what we agreed. Excellent.' Use positive reinforcement and acknowledgement to draw other students back on task without drawing attention to them; the 'off-task' student may well be drawn back to work by your attention to the hard work of his neighbour, just as a group who are wilting can be perked up through the example of another group. It is a gentler and less intrusive first step in sending the message but not confronting the behaviour immediately.

TOP TIP!

We are all motivated by praise and reward. It boosts our self-esteem; it makes us feel as if our efforts are recognised, that we are valued and that we've contributed positively to a given outcome. It is not the size or type of reward that is pivotal but the way that it is given. Reinforcing through additional comments at the end of a piece of work, a positive note home, sticker, certificate, positive referral ('Please go and show this work to Mr Glover, he will be so impressed at the detail and creativity of your story'), phone calls home and home visits, sticky notes subtly given to students who shy away from public praise. Triangulate your praise for those students who you are getting to know by passing it through a trusted teacher. Mark the moment to ensure students remember. To boost self-esteem and confidence and to give those who struggle to maintain appropriate behaviour a positive checkpoint to return to when things are bad.

When you praise Charlene for staying on task throughout the lesson you are doing so because she needs to hear the praise, not because you feel like giving it or have calculated that it would be fair to give it. Assuming that students don't need praise for doing what they 'should' be doing anyway is as dangerous as assuming that they know how to behave. How long will Charlene stay on task if her efforts are ignored? Multiply this by your class size and it is easy to see how the behaviour and work of classes can change radically between teachers who use praise and use positive reinforcement and those that do not. Remember not all students receive praise at home, just as not all students receive praise at school. Your interaction may not be memorable in your day but it may well be in hers.

Differentiating rewards

The skill in delivering rewards is through your differentiation. Younger children need rewards that are more immediate, older students can keep sight of rewards that are delayed until the end of the day, week or half term. For students who have learned negative or disruptive behaviour patterns smaller rewards may need to be given more often while a new pattern of behaviour is being established. This should be a temporary adjustment, and instead of rewarding them with a whole merit you might want to split the merit into five tallies or cut a Post-it note into five sections so that your differentiation for one does not become unfair on the rest. Students with low self-image and low self-esteem can find it difficult to accept praise in public or in private. The drip, drip of your consistent reinforcement will gradually (over a week, month, year for some) dissuade the student of their limiting self-belief. At the point at which the student asks you why you keep telling them that they are intelligent/able/skilled the door eases open to the possibility that your judgement may be right. A new behaviour cycle is rehearsed and the old one nudged into obscurity, a new expectation is established and a better relationship promoted.

Watch out for ...

- Using all of your positive energy on the first day. Being positive and delivering praise consistently and fairly throughout your working day can be exhausting. Praise is hard work at first, especially at the end of a long day with a challenging group, but it pays dividends in the short, long and medium term.

- Taking away praise/rewards. If you give students sincere praise and perhaps a reward for their hard work it should not be revoked. If they make poor choices afterwards give a verbal warning and then apply sanctions. There is no conflict in students receiving both.

- Using praise and reward as a bribe: they should only be provided after the positive behaviour.

→

Watch out for ... continued

- Slipping back into negatives when praise doesn't work the first time. Your students need to be convinced that your classroom is a consistently positive environment. This cannot be achieved in one day and your positive responses will need to become part of your teaching style and not an afterthought.

- Passing over those students who work quietly and consistently throughout your lessons. They deserve and need your acknowledgement and praise. Without it they may choose to gain attention by less positive means. Stand by the door as the students leave and catch those students you may have missed in the lesson.

Reflecting on practice

At 14 Shaun was a highly disruptive student. He was often absent and when he did appear he was keen to confirm his low opinion of his own abilities and the inadequacies of his teachers. In my lessons he was a problem and would stand at the side and watch more often than take part. There were rare flashes of limited enthusiasm that were not sustained. He demonstrated no more ability in Drama than any subject.

I felt sorry for his mother touring the teachers' tables at parents' evening being traumatised at every stop. All of Shaun's sins would be laid bare by teachers keen to vent their frustration at his continual disruption. By the time she reached my table at the end of the night she was resigned to listen to another litany of crimes and misdemeanours. I decided to concentrate on those moments when Shaun engaged in the lesson and left her feeling that it was not all lost and that he had some opportunities in Drama.

The following day Shaun came to see me and thanked me for what I had said to his mother. He recognised the fact that it was not wholly deserved but was interested to know why I thought he had some ability and potential in the subject. I explained it to him carefully and he listened.

Shaun's Head of Year came to see me the following week to discuss Shaun's part-time timetable and was keen to include Drama within it. He attended almost every lesson in two years, struggled with the coursework, as he had poor literacy skills, but engaged in practical work with real focus and enthusiasm. He attended theatre visits regularly and was blown away by mask work. Shaun only turned up for one examination at the end of Year 11 but he passed with a C grade and I will never forget the pride on his face when he came to collect his result.

The turning point of his self-belief came from that parents' evening.

Why not try this?

In the first week use the chart to record the positive and negative comments that you give to the class (ask a support teacher or observing colleague to help, if appropriate). Aim for a ratio of 3:1 positive to negative comments. Try to phrase a negative reaction in positive terms. For example, 'Thank you for sitting down so quickly; you will need the hand that is in Oliver's bag to write down the first key word' as opposed to, 'Stop doing that, you are supposed to be listening to me, how many times have I told you …' After the lesson note down any words or phrases that had a beneficial effect and those that you wish you hadn't said.

Positive comments	Negative comments
Tally total	Tally total ....
Words/phrases to watch out for	**Words/phrases to watch out for**

Key ideas summary

Key idea	Benefit for the teacher	Benefit for the students
The reward that most students value are relational, not material.	The teacher does not need to spend time and money searching for material rewards.	Students have positive interactions with teachers who are sincere with their praise and encouragement.
Acknowledgement and positive reinforcement create a positive ethos in the classroom.	Less time is spent on sanctions and disruptive behaviour. A continually positive ethos gathers momentum.	Students are able to gain the teacher's attention through fair means rather than foul!
Praise can be most effective when it is given with subtlety and discretion.	The teacher is able to reinforce positive behaviour without embarrassing individuals.	Students' communication with the teacher is more personal and effective.

Key idea	Benefit for the teacher	Benefit for the students
Aim to deliver praise that is sincere and individualised.	You begin to connect with your students and show them your pride in their achievements.	Students appreciate your praise; they recognise when you tailor your praise.
Praise is a far more effective behaviour-management tool than sanctions.	Enforcing sanctions is time-consuming and complicated. Teachers have a longer-term influence on behaviour using strategies for praise and reward.	Students are motivated by praise rather than sanctions.

Strategies for Primary, Secondary, FE and HE

Primary

Wanted: Stop and praise on sight

In your staff briefing on a Monday morning, try nominating one or two pupils who have made a determined effort to make good choices in their behaviour over the past week. Display their photographs so that everyone can recognise them, then ask every member of staff, teaching and non-teaching, to stop them and congratulate them when they see them around the site that day. Such a high level of personal and sincere verbal praise can make a lasting impact on the child, make the day stand out and sweep away negative preconceptions or damaging self-imposed labels. It also allows staff to openly admit that they discuss the behaviour of pupils in the staff room!

Secondary

Positive notes, texts, emails and calls

For me the catalyst to understanding rewards was the positive note and phone call home. Positive notes home connect home and school and have impact on a number of different levels. Parents see that appropriate behaviour ought to be rewarded, that the teacher is taking action to encourage good choices, and for some that their child is capable of controlling their behaviour. The wording is important. With a positive note you can shift the responsibility for material rewards to where it should be – the home:

'Alfie has made a great effort to behave well today. I am so pleased with his positive attitude to work and school. **If you would like to follow up with a reward at home it would be well deserved.**'

Once earned, the student is able to use the reward in different ways: firstly as a bargaining chip, 'Please can I go to the cinema/buy a book/play on the computer/kick my little brother? Look this note from my teacher says I am doing really well in class', secondly as a counter balance to the less welcome letters that begin, 'Dear Mrs Alfie, I am sorry to have to tell you that Alfie has been involved in vandalism/bullying/racketeering/small arms dealing, etc.', and finally as something just to keep under the pillow, look at and smile.

Parents would often berate me at parents evening with: 'You are the bloke who has covered my fridge in purple notes; it's costing me a fortune in Spiderman accessories!' Then they would smile and tell me how much they appreciated knowing when things were going well, how they enjoyed receiving positive phone calls on a Friday evening (a great start to the weekend) and how they had noticed an improved attitude in their child towards me, the work and the school. The parents also recognised how their child was becoming a skilled negotiator and how the positive contact had a currency in the home.

FE and HE

Human beings of all ages are motivated by positive reinforcement, praise and reward. Don't assume that your students have grown too old or too independent to value praise. Remember, it is not what you give but the way that you give it. I would regularly sit and mark the work of Year 7 students and be harangued by my A-level group for the gorilla stickers and elephant stamps. When I pointed out that they were too old for such things the reply would always be 'WE Are Not!', followed by arguments about which amusing animal was the most valued. Your students also like reinforcement that is written: at the end of a piece of work, on a card, quick note or email. They re-read it, reflect on it and value it. If you are worried about giving your older students or adult learners too much praise, just think, when was the last time you gave that student who comes every day and works as hard as she can a written reinforcement?

30 days to make a change

Think about the changes that you would like to make in how you motivate students and reinforce behaviour. This might relate to an individual student, class or context. Commit to the new strategies for 30 days to allow them to embed into practice and your own teaching style.

In 30 days I will walk into work and ....

....

....

....

Make a commitment to try some of the strategies that have been suggested in this chapter.

My personal resolutions are:

1 _____   Review date _____
2 _____   Review date _____
3 _____   Review date _____

Reconciliation v retribution: the art of applying effective sanctions

'Punishment hardens and numbs, it produces obstinacy, it sharpens the sense of alienation and strengthens the power of resistance.'

(Friedrich Wilhelm Nietzsche)

The principle

Your sanctions must be graduated, applied consistently and gently and leave the students' self-esteem intact. Students need to be spoken to privately whenever possible; your approach should be non-threatening, with the discussion at eye level. Sanctions must address the behaviour and not the personality of the individual. **When students choose to break rules that have been taught and made explicit through displays on the classroom walls, sanctions need to be consistently applied. Effective sanctions are consequences, not revenge or punishment to demean.**

The practice

If punitive sanctions actually changed behaviour there would be no reoffending, the police would be eating donuts, you wouldn't be reading this book and I would be out of a job. When sanctions are used to reinforce the lines of appropriate behaviour, to repair trust and make agreements for future conduct, then they can have a sustained impact. When they are personal retribution, revenge or born from an emotional response they are remembered for the wrong reasons.

Don't be surprised when students break your rules and rituals. Expect it, plan for it and use it as an opportunity to teach and encourage better choices.

Being spoken to about your behaviour in front of your peers is at best tense and at worst terrifying. Just check your own reaction the next time you are beeped at for some minor driving error, or admonished at the dinner table by your partner in front of friends. Being spoken to about your personal conduct in public is embarrassing; having it shouted across a room full of your peers can be humiliating and more often than not elicit a defensive reaction. So it goes with students.

Private and discreet application of sanctions reduces the chance of challenge and confrontation. The audience is removed and conversation is quieter and calmer.

Non-verbal

There are many non-verbal ways in which you can communicate with the students about their choices before approaching them and intervening. Your non-verbal cues may not be immediately or accurately understood by a new group of students and you may need to be explicit about the techniques that you are using. For example, 'When I am speaking to the class and I stand next to your table I am giving you a chance to check your choices before I need to stop and give you a verbal warning.' When the class can read your non-verbal cues, your initial response can be discreet yet still work. You can begin to manage minor infringements without being inter- rupted or having to stop what you are saying to the class.

For many, graduated sanctions start with a warning, for others the suggestion of the consequence is given earlier and with more subtlety. Just as you pick up your stickers/positive notes/stars, etc. to encourage appropriate behaviour, so you might gently waft your warning card near Layla's table, ask how her surname is spelt as you thumb your referral sheet or feign humorous shock and surprise at her choice of behaviour that lightens the moment. Teachers who launch into delivering sanctions at the first sniff of inappropriate behaviour often find themselves at the top of the sanctions ladder too quickly with nowhere else to go. It is easy to design a system that leads to the cliff edge of exclusion quickly; one that leaves even eight year olds having exhausted every level of sanction. It takes more consistent effort to inch slowly up the ladder and each day start from the bottom again.

Effective sanctions for serial rule breakers are those which allow time for re-establishing expectations, re-chalking the boundary lines, repairing trust and making a commitment for the next lesson/day/10 minutes. Punitive sanctions satisfy the desire for mild revenge in the unenlightened, detach the punishment from the original rule break and make children resentful. Lines (yes they are still being used, widely), detentions that are not used to discuss behaviour, loss of time that is delegated to others, repeated sanctions that are subsumed into the schedule of the child's day (how many children spend every lunchtime inside yet their behaviour is the same?), humiliation and disproportionate sanctions ('Right, that is the second time I have asked you to sit down, go and wait outside the headteacher's office') don't set the right model or have a positive impact on behaviour.

In many classrooms sanctions have become bargaining chips, 'If I work hard for the next 10 minutes can you let me go out to play?' is a tempting deal, particularly if you have been battling to get Kylie to emerge from under the table since she arrived. However, if you give children the idea that 30 minutes of poor behaviour can be outweighed by 10 minutes of effort, then expect them to seek this deal more often. Similarly, threatening to withdraw a reward because of subsequent poor behaviour means that even positive consequences are negotiable. Skilled negotiators in Year 4, who may already experience inconsistency at home, will protest at your inconsistency in the morning and use it to their advantage in the afternoon.

Some children want to see how cross you get the higher up the sanctions list they go; they are used to sanctions being accompanied with a side dish of anger or a dressing of frustration. Removing the negative emotion from the delivery of the sanction is difficult in the to and fro of the day but is more than worth the extra effort. If Riana constantly gets excitement from your angry face, the adrenalin of raised voices and the peer admiration for making an adult go red then she is encouraged to see the connection between her behaviour and how it affects your emotional state. Deliver your sanctions with a cold, bland, emotionless script. The sanction must be the discouragement and not the force of your emotion. In schools and colleges where a consistent effort is made to keep sanctions and emotions separate, children become more resigned to the sanction and less likely to fight against it.

TOP TIP!

Six ways to add impact to your sanctions

- *Design them so they can be delivered as soon as possible after the event. It is not the severity of the sanction that has most impact but the speed with which it is delivered*
- *Once given, don't remove a sanction. Some children will get the idea that they are negotiable*
- *Keep your response rational; indifference is better than indignation*
- *Avoid passing sanctions for others to execute. Use the time to reconcile, repair and reset expectations*
- *Tread carefully with public sanctions; private is preferable*
- *Beware of 'hovering'; deliver the sanction and leave the child to think.*

Over time you will be able to build up a range of non-verbal cues that allow students' poor choices to be addressed subtly within the 'flow' of your teaching. It is these proactive and preventative techniques that are so hard to observe in effective teachers; as they are refined they become so discreet and embedded in the teaching style that they are barely noticeable.

Why not try this?

- Stand or sit next to the student as you continue to address the class: it will encourage them to check their behaviour
- Gain eye contact that gently says, 'Come on, let's get back to work', or a stronger look that indicates that you are aware of and disapprove of the behaviour
- Mention the name of a student drifting off to refocus their attention
- Feign shock and surprise at the student's choice of behaviour
- Refer to a strong model of the student's previous good behaviour to bring them back on task
- Use agreed signals, such as miming a writing motion with your hand or placing palms together to ask for books to be closed
- Indicate their chairs with an open palm to invite them to sit down
- Stand next to the charts that display the learning rituals and rules and combine eye contact with a hand on the chart to send a clear message.

Unless it is a serious incident, e.g., verbal abuse directed at the teacher or violent behaviour which endangers the class, your first sanction should be a verbal warning. Take a moment to prepare what you are going to say to the student. Approach the student calmly and gently and get down to their eye level. Explain that the behaviour witnessed is contrary to the rules and that you are giving them a warning. Then focus on the learning that you expect to see the student engaged in.

If the student tries to divert the conversation or bring in the behaviour of another student, you can say, 'I understand what you are saying: we are talking about ...', or, 'I hear that: I am talking about your choices.' You are acknowledging his point but returning the focus back to the undesirable behaviour.

Refocusing the conversation

When students try to argue, shift the blame or divert the conversation you can either:

● **Calmly and gently repeat the line during which you have been interrupted.**

This encourages the student to realise that you will not be diverted from the conversation you are leading. The more calmly assertive you are in delivering this repeat the more effective it will be. Try slowing down the request the second time you repeat it and using gentle eye contact to reinforce.

Or:

● **Use an appropriate refocusing line to bring the conversation back to the script.**

This allows the student to feel as though they are being listened to and avoids conversational cul-de-sacs.

Student	Adult
'It wasn't me'	'I hear what you are saying ...'
'But they were doing the same thing'	'I understand ...'
'I was only ...'	'Maybe you were ... and yet ...'
'You are not being fair'	'Yes, sometimes I may appear unfair ...'
'It's boring'	'Yes, you may think it boring ... and yet ...'
'You are a ... (name calling)	'There may be some truth in that ...' (*with follow up served cold!*) or 'I am sorry that you are having a bad day'

'Out-line'

If the conversation is becoming unproductive, use:

'I am stopping this conversation now. I am going to walk away and give you a chance to think about your conduct. I know that when I come back we can have a polite, productive conversation.'

Finish your discussion by referring to the student's previous good behaviour, 'Last lesson your detailed descriptive paragraph was a result of hard work; try and get back to those good choices', and leave them feeling positive about the rest of the lesson. You may even add some surprise at his poor choices, 'Dan, it is unlike you to need to go down the sanctions route; you are not someone who usually makes poor choices ...'. Then walk away and look away. Turn your attention to the rest of the class and catch someone doing the right thing. Give the student the space to calm down, consider his next choice and act upon it. After a couple of minutes, check that the student who received the sanction is back on task and give him a gentle acknowledgement that you appreciate his better choice. If he is still choosing to break the rules, return and apply your second sanction (often a request for him to see you after class to discuss his behaviour choices) with the same consistent, personal and calm approach.

Watch out for ...

- 'Hovering' by a student after you have applied a sanction. The student needs time and space to make better choices about her behaviour and your continued proximity makes this very difficult. I have observed teachers who have a graduated sanctions list and, by standing over a student, manage to apply all five sanctions in 30 seconds. The student feels humiliated and resentful. Her personal space has been invaded and she has not been given a fair chance to change her behaviour. A small rule-break suddenly escalates into a full-blown confrontation that does not meet the needs of the student or teacher.

- Holding grudges. Each lesson should be a clean sheet for students. Poor choices in the previous lesson should either be dealt with in the interim or at another time. Students need to know that they have not been labelled by their previous poor choices.

- Giving a sanction and then taking it away. Regardless of how many good choices the student makes after a sanction is applied, you should not remove the sanction. Your students need to understand that there are consequences to certain choices and these are not negotiable. You should reward good choices even if they follow poor ones. It is not unusual for some students to leave the classroom with both.

Reflecting on practice

Instant sanctions with added impact

Working with students who were struggling to control their own behaviour meant that I rarely had lunch alone. I had discovered that having 'guests' to lunch was a highly effective sanction. My acknowledgement, praise and positive reinforcement had most effect when it was immediate. My sanctions needed to match.

For these students the more delayed the sanction the less they associated it with the inappropriate behaviour. Sanctions would simply be an inconvenience in their school week, swiftly integrated into their routine. As a student I remember this well and accepted detention as part of my timetable rather than connecting it with the original behaviour. For me (and a number of my friends) the school day would finish at 4.30 rather than 3.30 and rather than adjust my behaviour I came to accept a later finishing time as an occupational hazard.

For sanctions to be most effective they need to be served immediately and be designed to disrupt the student's plan for the day. Holding students at break, lunch and after school works best when lessons fall before their free time or when you are able to collect them before their free time begins. They connect the behaviour directly with the sanction and when their carefully protected and planned free time is compromised they begin to check their behaviour with more care.

Diligent application of impositions (extra work to be completed at home, signed by parents and delivered before school the following morning) can have a similar effect, but, 'You are in detention a week on Wednesday' is so far removed from the original behaviour that it is questionable whether it really has any influence on future behaviour choices. With students who persistently break the rules you will need to negotiate with parents so that you are able to apply sanctions on the same day as the incident. Students will remind you that you need to give 24 hours' notice before a detention can be served; you can remind them that you have a prior agreement with their parents, pick up the phone and get immediate clearance.

Why not try this?

Read the sample structure for intervention and fill in the gaps with examples of your own language using vocabulary you are comfortable with. Learn and practise the structure for applying the sanctions until you are comfortable with the sequence. Don't leave out section 'c', as the strongest model for the behaviour that you expect is the student's previous good choices. This structure is also extremely useful when delivering praise (I have included it in italics). In both instances you need to have a structure for opening, developing and closing the interaction efficiently, leaving both parties with their self-esteem intact.

Sample structure for intervention

Delivering warning/sanction

Delivering praise

(a) Gentle approach, personal, non-threatening, eye level, eye contact.

(b) State the behaviour that was observed and which ritual/rule it contravenes.

(b) State exactly what it is that you are praising and why.

Example: ....

(c) Tell the student what the sanction is. Refer to previous good behaviour/ learning as a model for desired behaviour.

(c) Tell the student what the reward is.

Example: ....

(d) Tell the student what will happen if he continues with this approach to learning.

Example: ....

(e) Tell him that his choice was poor and he needs to make better choices.

(e) Thank him for making the right choices.

Example: ....

(f) Walk away from the student; allow him time to make a better choice. If he is back on task give him appropriate praise and/or acknowledgement.

(g) Scan the room and catch somebody following the routine.

Do not discuss consequences in learning time. Use 'I understand' or 'I hear what you are saying' and return to your original point.

Do not allow yourself to be drawn away from the conversation you want to have.

Recognise secondary behaviours and avoid 'chasing' them (see Chapter 8 on managing confrontation).

Key ideas summary

Key idea	Benefit for the teacher	Benefit for the students
When students break the rules use it as an opportunity to teach them about better choices.	The focus for the interaction is learning about improving choices rather than simply attacking behaviour.	Students are involved in negotiating future expectations rather than just answering for their current behaviour.
Apply sanctions in private whenever possible.	Public confrontations are avoided.	Students have no audience to play to or react for.
Integrate a range of non-verbal cues into the flow of your teaching to prevent inappropriate behaviour.	The teacher is proactive in maintaining the students' attention and does not have to keep stopping to deal with students interrupting.	Students are redirected back to the activity without a fuss or their behaviour being advertised to the rest of the class.
Use a planned framework for intervening and applying sanctions.	The teacher is able to direct and control the direction of the conversation without prompting confrontation.	Students know what to expect, recognise the structure of the intervention and may decide not to argue.
Use students' previous good behaviour as a model for desired behaviour.	The interaction is softened after the sanction is delivered. The conversation ends on a positive note.	Students fully understand the required standards of behaviour.
Use instant sanctions whenever possible.	Teachers can use the time to repair relationships and reinforce appropriate choices while the incident is current. Less time is spent chasing students who are avoiding sanctions for past misdemeanours.	Students are keen to avoid sanctions that eat into their social time without notice.

Strategies for Primary, Secondary, FE and HE

Primary

If you want to separate a child from the group for a time out, match the time with the age of the child in minutes, e.g., for a 5 year old, 5 minutes and for a 10 year old, 10 minutes. Your sanction is the surprised and sudden nature of the separation, not the length of it. Reintegrate the student on your own terms with a clear view of what will happen if the behaviour recurs. Use the same ritual for the conversations, one that is utterly predictable, safe, and yet certain. At the end of the conversation check for understanding with, 'So when we finish talking tell me precisely what you are going to do.'

Secondary

Names on the board with ticks and crosses make one student's behaviour everyone's business. With older students, systems that publicly highlight behaviour can in themselves be a catalyst for disruptive behaviour: students trying to covertly wipe their names off the board, students laughing at the misfortune of others, public arguments about level of sanction applied, etc. I know that in large classes it is difficult to keep every interaction private, but as far as possible the sanctions should be kept between you and the student. It is important that students understand where they are on the hierarchy of consequences, but it can be divisive if others know this information.

FE and HE

Although you will have a structure of consequences in the institution, it is important to also have a clear view of the sanctions that operate within your classroom or practical area. If you only have the high-level sanctions of taking away the EMA or writing a written referral to the tutor, you are missing a trick. Regardless of the age of your students they need to be sure that those who disrupt the work of others will have consequences applied. You might decide to have just three, such as 1. Warning; 2. Minute after the lesson; 3. 15 minute lunchtime meeting.

30 days to make a change

Think about the changes that you would like to make in how you motivate students and reinforce behaviour. This might relate to an individual student, class or context. Commit to the new strategies for 30 days to allow them to embed into practice and your own teaching style.

In 30 days I will walk into work and ....

....

....

....

Make a commitment to try some of the strategies that have been suggested in this chapter.

My personal resolutions are:

1 _____   Review date _____

2 _____   Review date _____

3 _____   Review date _____

Part
2

Advanced behaviour-management strategies

Managing confrontation with flair: the 'win, win'

'The real menace about dealing with a five-year-old is that in no time at all you begin to sound like a five-year-old.'

(Jean Kerr)

The principle

There will be times when, regardless of how calmly and reasonably you apply sanctions, you find yourself in a confrontation with a student. There will also be times when you are confronted by a student, without warning, for no explicit reason.

The way you manage the confrontation has a direct effect on its outcome, even if the outcome is not an instant solution or a perfect one. A carefully managed confrontation with a student can have positive outcomes even if the beginning of the conversation is a difficult experience for both parties. At all times remember who the adult is, model the behaviour you

expect and enjoy skillfully managing the situation to meet the best needs of your students.

The practice

Confrontations can happen in an instant and often when you are least expecting them. You need to work to keep your own emotions in check throughout, to protect yourself and the student. I have had many weekends tarnished by guilt after saying the wrong thing to the wrong student late on a Friday afternoon. Stepping back and taking time to consider the most appropriate response is vital if you are to avoid such mistakes.

Your response to the first signs of a confrontation sets the rhythm for the rest of the discussion. Change your focus from being the speaker to being the listener. While you are listening look at your own body language and soften it, take a step back, sit down on a table, lower your hands, indicate with open palms rather than pointed fingers, remove any aggressive tightening of the facial muscles and then prepare what you are going to say. Control your tone, squeeze out any anger, sarcasm and irritation and replace it with care, kindness and sincere empathy.

We usually know what our opening sentence in an escalating confrontation will be but few plan beyond it. Work through what you are going to say in response, how you will say it, how you are going to end the conversation, and stick to your plan. As with applying sanctions, students need to know that they are being listened to. Use 'I hear what you are saying', 'I understand' and 'I'm sorry that you are having a bad day'. You will find that the confrontation needs the fuel of an equally confrontational response to keep it escalating. If your response is to listen, and keep listening (whenever possible), until the student has finished and take immediate steps to de-escalate, using appropriate physical and verbal language, any aggression will be short-lived. Most violent or aggressive incidents are entirely preventable. Through skilled management of the situation you can come away with your dignity and the dignity of the student intact.

Some students have learned that by quickly escalating an intervention into a confrontation they can avoid responsibility for the original behaviour. This can be a shocking and seemingly illogical tactic but for the student it makes absolute sense. The learned behaviour is that the faster and more instant the escalation the less responsibility for the original rule break. The student is 'running' away from responsibility as fast as possible, perhaps trying to tempt your emotional response so that they can blame you for the incident. View the escalation as a tactic or trick and you can stay calm and focused on the original behaviour. Regardless as to how serious the escalation, always bring the student back to repair the original damage. If the student escalates, confronts and then runs away, make sure the student is safe, record what was said and make a commitment to bring the student back to the original behaviour when things are calm.

Don't try to solve all confrontations instantly. You may need to walk away and take time and advice on how to resolve the situation. You may need to listen, record and then refer on to a senior colleague. When students have sworn, threatened and physically confronted me, I never improved the situation through an aggressive or emotional response.

TOP TIP!

As soon as possible after the incident make a detailed chronological written record of what happened and who said what. This is not only a useful reflective (and cathartic) action but also clarifies the incident for senior colleagues and parents. If confrontations happen with some frequency, carry a Dictaphone or use the voice recorder on your mobile phone to make an accurate record of the incident immediately afterwards (not during as it can inflame an already tense situation). If appropriate, encourage the student to record their version of events. For younger students, call it a 'Think Sheet' with key questions: 'What happened to make you feel wound up? What did you do about this? What do you think you should do next time?' Use a cold comparison of the two versions to learn more about the effect of your actions and reactions on the student.

Anger management

Intensive anger management coaching and counselling can have a marked effect on student behaviour; but providing a diluted version for half-an-hour a week to groups of students has little chance of success. Educational psychologists identify this as a growing issue for schools who think they are providing appropriate intervention but are unable to give it the time and financial commitment that it requires to have a measurable effect. Students pick up on the fact that the school has given such courses a low priority, and are aware of the frustration that teachers feel when students are removed from lessons to attend the course. The intervention can all too easily be undermined, cue students: 'It's not my fault, I've got anger management problems', and teachers: 'He just uses it as an excuse not to work.' In some cases anger management courses have been misused as a poorly resourced 'final chance' before permanent exclusion: 'He's been on the course, now we can put him out.'

For anger management training to succeed certain conditions and principles need to be in place:

● Courses are given a high priority by all staff

- They are well-resourced and delivered by trained specialists
- The course is intensive and one-to-one in the first instance
- Training is tailored to the needs of the individual student (not simply a series of worksheets)
- The student commits to the course
- The parents commit to the course and are closely involved and clearly communicated with
- All teachers are given a clear rationale for the intervention
- The management of the student is not delegated to the anger management course leader, 'Well if she can't help him I'm not even going to try'
- Students are not allowed or encouraged to blame their inappropriate choices on 'anger management problems'.

Some students enjoy a confrontation with a teacher. It can be an opportunity for adrenaline-fuelled interlude into his otherwise uneventful day and is quickly forgotten. For others it is frightening and shocking. It can damage the teacher–student relationship irrevocably. Your careful management of confrontation can quell the former and protect the latter.

TOP TIP!

Students, like teachers, have a sophisticated armoury with which to defend themselves when confronted. A secondary behaviour might be the smirk that glides across the face of a student who is supposed to be looking ashamed, the door that is slammed after the student is sent from the room or the muttering as you walk away. These behaviours can attract a stronger response than the initial incident. They are 'chase me' behaviours designed to get an emotional response from the teacher. Don't ignore them but do choose the right time to address them, when the student has calmed down.

Watch out for ...

- Allowing the discussion to be diverted. There are common diversionary tactics that can extend a ten-second confrontation into an hour-long discussion. They usually start with, 'I don't like this class and my dad says it's a waste of time anyway' or, 'What's the point of History?' Use, 'I understand ...' or, 'I hear what you are saying ...' to get the conversation back on track.
- Bringing up past misdemeanours or using as a model the example of siblings or other students: 'Your brother never behaved like this.'

Watch out for ... continued

- Invading students' personal space. Students may feel threatened and become aggressive if their personal space is continually violated. Personal space is circular (360°), cultural and critical.

- Offering unsolicited advice or criticism when discussing choices with students: 'If I were you ...' or, 'Do you want to carry on being stupid or have you grown up now?'

Reflecting on practice

Violent behaviour: fights breaking out in lessons

Your skilled management of behaviour and knowledge of individual students should minimise physical confrontation between students in lesson time. The culture of mutual trust and regard that you are building will go a long way to reduce the chances of violent conduct. With some extremely volatile students 'Hands off' is a useful rule to use while they are learning appropriate behaviour for the classroom. 'Hands off' means 'no touch' in anger or without permission. This has two benefits: it enables you to give a clear command when you see physical confrontation beginning and deters those who poke/flick/push others in fun and provoke a violent reaction. With students who are used to this terminology, the first flames of aggression can often be extinguished with a loud, low-toned and controlled assertive call of 'DANIEL, HANDS OFF.'

There will be occasions, however, when fights break out. Regardless of your size your first move should not be to intervene physically but to send a responsible student to get the nearest adult and in the same breath begin intervening verbally by giving clear instructions to the participants. At this point it is too late to start telling them that you are 'going to get Mr Hopkins' or that 'You will be excluded for this.' Your commands should be clear and unassailable: 'Rizwan, put your hands down and step back' or 'Julie McManon, stand by my desk.' If the students are young enough that you can safely intervene physically before another adult arrives, then you should do so. As you pull them apart, do so by the shoulder or by holding down the arms of one child by the upper arm, so as to keep their arms held to the side. Remember to keep a strong check on your heightened emotional state and ensure that the force you use is the absolute minimum required. Keep talking to the students while you are separating them, explaining what you are doing and telling them what you want them to do next: 'You are not fighting in my classroom', 'I am holding your arms down to stop you hurting anyone',

→

'Sit down in the chair.' If you are concerned about restraining students, then the DCSF document 'Guidance on the use of restrictive physical interventions for staff working with children and adults 2002' is useful.

With older and stronger students, or those who have lost all emotional control, intervening physically can carry significant risk. If you are in any doubt wait until support arrives and evacuate the room for the safety of other students and leave the door open. I have witnessed some nasty fights with older teenagers and we have had to wait for five or six teachers to arrive before we could be sure of intervening safely. Without support it is all too easy to get involved in the physical to-and-fro and find yourself being hit, using excessive force, restraining one student while the other takes the opportunity for some 'free hits', or being perceived as showing favouritism to one student or the other.

Unfortunately, intervening physically carries risks, but so does standing by and watching. While the law does not protect teachers, we have to trust our judgement.

Why not try this?

Plan your responses to confrontation using the chart below. Refer to them throughout the week, adopting them where appropriate. Measure the students' reaction to them carefully.

Responses to confrontation

Your first reaction to an escalating confrontation:

....

While the student is speaking you will:

....

When you want to exit the confrontation you will say:

'...'

As soon as the confrontation has finished you will:

....

When sufficient time has elapsed you will:

....

Key ideas summary

Key idea	Benefit for the teacher	Benefit for the students
Take a step back and listen rather than speak.	The teacher has more time to deliver a considered response; the confrontation is not fuelled from two sides.	Students learn that teachers will not engage in aggressive confrontation; they experience a positive model of behaviour at first hand.
Think carefully about what you are going to say and how you are going to say it.	With more considered use of language the teacher has more chance of calming aggression and leading the way out of confrontation.	Students hear simple, impartial instructions and receive non-verbal cues to calm down.
Don't look for instant solutions.	The teacher is not under pressure to improvise an instant resolution and may move the discussion to a more appropriate time/ location.	Students are given time to consider their behaviour; they know that 'knee jerk' or unfair reactions are less likely.
Write a detailed and accurate record as soon as possible.	The teacher has a reliable record of what was said, what took place and who else was involved.	The student has the time and space to reflect on the incident before it is discussed.

Strategies for Primary, Secondary, FE and HE

Primary

Younger children's confrontation is mostly tantrum with occasional direct insult. Take up time is vital. Teach the children that they do not get your attention while they are shouting and protesting. Walk away, wait until they are calm and record the time that they owe you for their outburst. The message must be clear, 'That behaviour may work elsewhere but it will *never* work here'.

Secondary

You can win a confrontation without winning the immediate verbal battle. You can teach appropriate behaviour by how you respond, in fact your own behaviour will be in sharp focus throughout. How you behave in front of the aggressor is as important as how you behave in front of your audience. Rehearse your 'outline' so that you can remove yourself from the confrontation before it escalates further, 'I can see that you are upset, I am going to walk away and we can talk about this when we are both calm'.

FE and HE

Confrontation is more likely to be between students than it is between staff and students. If you are working with particularly volatile groups, make sure you have a rehearsed procedure for calling on support/security. Talk to the security team and agree a plan with them.

30 days to make a change

Think about the changes that you would like to make in how you manage behaviour. This might relate to an individual student, class or context. Commit to the new strategies for 30 days to allow them to embed into practice and your own teaching style.

In 30 days I will walk into work and ....

....

....

....

Make a commitment to try some of the strategies that have been suggested in this chapter.

My personal resolutions are:

1 _____   Review date _____

2 _____   Review date _____

3 _____   Review date _____

Pivotal moments in hooking hard to reach students

'I don't know if I have the right attitude for the workplace.'

(Bill Hicks)

The principle

Students with challenging behaviour select the lessons that they are going to disrupt and the teachers they are going to frustrate. They find it harder to maintain their aggression and inappropriate behaviour with teachers that they trust. There are actions you can take to develop in a proactive way a professional and trusting relationship with an individual student and so reduce their desire for conflict and confrontation in your lesson. With particularly challenging students who persistently disrupt

your lesson and fail to respond to your hierarchy of sanctions, the only way you are going to effect a change in behaviour and teacher–student relationships is to be proactive in developing a trusting relationship.

The practice

It's not about trying to get down with the kids. Get the image of the teacher in a baseball cap skipping up to a group of gnarled Year 11s with a 'Yo mothers wagwan, dis new Phil Collins is safe man' out of your head. It is certainly not what I am suggesting, although it would be fun to watch.

TOP TIP!

Try not to think in terms of gaining the respect or friendship of the student, but about gaining their trust. Trust thrives when two people like each other. It certainly helps if you can get on but trust can and does exist strongly between people who have no real personal connection. It is your responsibility to build trust with all students; regardless of whether you like them or not. It is better to spend your time working on this premise rather than waiting for the students to decide that they are going to bestow their trust on you. Some colleagues will busy themselves with mourning the loss of children's respect for teachers. Unfortunately it is nearly always a very dull conversation, prompted by teachers who don't really like children, that has no resolution; stay well away.

Choose your opportunities to build a relationship with a student carefully. Perhaps wait until you see the student away from their peer group, or open up a dialogue when the student appears relaxed and unguarded. You may choose to wait until you find a situation that is not pressured or time-limited. Aim for little and often rather than launching into a lengthy and involved conversation.

Remember, your intervention may be unwelcome at first. Your aim is to gently persuade the student that you are committed to building trust. Be prepared for your approaches to be rejected. The student may be testing you to see how committed to developing the relationship you really are. He may not welcome any informal conversation with you because it is easier for him to deal with a conflict than a relationship of trust. Or, quite simply, he may have decided that all teachers need to be given a wide berth.

Once you have levered the door open to a positive relationship the hard work begins and you may need to go an extra few miles, at times it might be uncomfortable. Start sending positive messages home or through the tutor. Sandwich bad news about the day in between positive observations, phone up, send positive notes, hang it, ask the parents if you can come for a cup of tea. Proactively build a relationship with the home and with the student. Refuse to give up and refuse to give in. Expect colleagues to shake their heads and tell you that you are not a social worker. Ask for support from others but never delegate your responsibility. On a daily basis go out of your way to build positive relationships with the students many adults would give a wide berth to. It is important that they grow to trust you, to like you, to lean on you.

Building a lasting professional relationship that meets the needs of the teacher and student is a balancing act that requires the skill and experience of a high-wire act. Any fool can befriend a student at the expense of their own dignity, 'Call me Bob'; at the expense of other members of staff, 'I don't much like him either'; or at the expense of their own pocket, 'Take this golden iPod as a reward/gift/ bribe for your efforts.' A relationship that is based on a pseudo 'friendship' can jog along quite happily until the moment where the frustrations of learning need to be addressed, when deadlines must be kept and when confidence wobbles. Most of us accept our friends for what they are without attempting to draw the boundaries for them. In a learning environment boundaries must be drawn and friendship blurs the boundaries, sending mixed messages to your students.

Mutual trust and respect are earned not bestowed. There are learning and behaviour boundaries that you expect your students to adhere to. So it goes with teacher–pupil relationships.

For some students you will need to define your boundaries and expectations very clearly. This is particularly pertinent on trips and visits where the expectations can change as more of your personal routines are revealed. In a digital context, where more private communication is the norm, these boundaries may need to be drawn with a thicker line. MySpace, Bebo, Twitter and Facebook are for friends, not for teachers and current students.

Building mutual trust with pupils is not just a core responsibility of the teacher but is the foundation for the fourth R: Rapport. Seasoned professionals know that the key is to be friendly and not friends, to be honest but not reveal personal lives, and to be open but not transparent.

Over time, try to find a way into the student's interests: it may be enough to simply listen, although you may choose to find some shared knowledge or experience. There will be times when you need to seek out the student to deliver a sanction or follow up on an incident in a lesson. In the early days do not try to use this opportunity to develop your relationship with the student: you may send mixed messages. As the relationship develops and you gain a better understanding of each other you may be able to switch between formal and informal registers and still get your message across.

Use meetings with parents to find out a little more about the student's home life, interests and motivations. Weigh up the advantages of accompanying school trips against the obvious disruption to your personal life. Teachers who accompany trips abroad or long weekends away (Outward Bound, Duke of Edinburgh Award, etc.) often cannot sustain their formal 'mask' that they use in the classroom and are forced to reveal more of their personality to the group; disruptive students have the same trouble trying to hide the gentler sides of their character. Teachers return from such trips often reporting that their relationship with individuals has changed and developed. They have been more open with each other, without the screen of institutional formality. They shared experiences which can be used to build the relationship on returning to the classroom. Students may not immediately demonstrate their appreciation for teachers who invest time in extra-curricular activities, but they do recognise the level of commitment and are more likely to give you their trust.

I always loved such trips and volunteered enthusiastically for D of E activities, skiing in Italy, weekends on Scout camps in Coventry, etc. For me, the benefits outweigh hassles of the paperwork, time away from the rest of your life, preparation of cover work, giving up your weekend, etc. You see the students for who they really are – young people learning about a world that is bigger and more exciting than anything the confines of the institution tries to replicate.

Watch out for …

- Speaking publicly about conversations you have had privately with students. There is nothing guaranteed to break trust faster than blurting out details of informal conversations in the staffroom or in front of other students.
- Meeting with students in a closed classroom. Obviously you will need to use your professional judgement and knowledge of the student, but it is always better to meet with students in a public space – the library, dining hall, reception area.

Disclosure

You cannot and never should offer or guarantee pupils unconditional confidentiality. A personal disclosure might occur without warning and when you least expect it. If you suspect that the student is about to disclose sexual abuse, pregnancy, criminal acts, domestic violence, self-harm, forced marriage or any sensitive information that you think needs to be referred, ask them to pause. I find the following script useful:

'I'm sorry to stop you but this is a sensitive issue and I need to tell the Principal/ Headteacher (or "named officer"). You can either stop talking to me now and talk to the Principal/Headteacher or talk to me and then I will speak to her. I cannot keep this information confidential. It is not my decision.'

Explain to the student that whilst you appreciate the trust they are giving you there are certain things that you must tell others about. It is part of your responsibility and legal duty as a teacher.

Once the student has listened to you and had an opportunity to think about what you have said they may still wish to disclose sensitive information to you. The DCSF guidance here is useful:

> 'Listen carefully without jumping to conclusions, asking leading questions or putting words into their mouth. Write a record of the conversation as soon as possible distinguishing clearly between fact, observation, allegation and opinion, noting any action taken in cases of possible abuse and signing and dating the note.'

> (DCSF, 2004, *Safeguarding Children in Education*)

Explain to the student what you will be doing with the information. Reassure them at this stage it will only be one other member of staff who knows, and that the student will be involved in what happens next. As soon as possible, meet with the designated person or 'named officer' within the school who has responsibility for child protection. If you are unsure as to who this is, go directly to the Headteacher. Thereafter it is not your responsibility to investigate the matter further and if there are repeated disclosures you must repeat the same process.

I have been involved in many cases of personal disclosure and students have rarely been surprised when I stopped them and reminded them of my responsibility to refer the information. In some cases they wanted to release the information and had calculated that telling a trusted teacher was a controlled way of doing so. Sometimes what I thought was a disclosure, particularly on drug and alcohol abuse, was fairly common knowledge outside the school. Then there were those times when the disclosure was sudden and extreme and urgent. In all cases I am sure that I have acted in the best interests of the child (even if in the short term it has not improved matters) by following the procedures above.

These guidelines are designed to protect the student, yourself and any evidence. They are not a reason for not offering support and guidance to students, and on lesser matters being a confidante. Just as guidance on touch is not designed to stop the to-and-fro of human interaction, so the guidance on safeguarding children should not be viewed as a reason to stop talking and building relationships.

Reflecting on practice

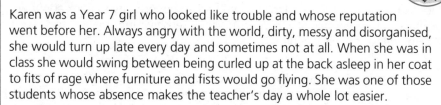

Two sides

Karen was a Year 7 girl who looked like trouble and whose reputation went before her. Always angry with the world, dirty, messy and disorganised, she would turn up late every day and sometimes not at all. When she was in class she would swing between being curled up at the back asleep in her coat to fits of rage where furniture and fists would go flying. She was one of those students whose absence makes the teacher's day a whole lot easier.

Complaints from staff would flow in and I would leave messages for parents, counsel and confine Karen and stave off continual requests for her to be excluded. She had recently moved from the local primary school, who had reported a deterioration in her behaviour and personal hygiene towards the end of her last term. In my numerous discussions with Karen I tried my best to develop a relationship with her, but she wouldn't let me in. She had created a 'front' for school and she was determined not to let it fall.

Some more urgent messages for contact with parents were sent and replied to by letter: Karen insisted that her parents were working all hours and simply didn't have time to come in to school. This written exchange was not improving the situation and phone calls to the house were answered by the grandmother who could offer no help. I resolved to visit the house after work, albeit uninvited.

I arrived at the house and Karen answered; she was not angry but very insistent that she had some things to tell me. As her parents were not in, we agreed to meet during tutor period the next day. It transpired that Karen's parents had left the house some five months ago. She was caring full-time for her elderly and ill grandmother, which included broken nights and nights with no sleep. She was also running the house, cooking, shopping and cleaning when there was time. She was angry because her parents had left but most of all she was tired. With so much responsibility at home it is not surprising that school was very low on the list of priorities. However, the fact that she arrived at school at all was something of an achievement. With additional support Karen managed to get some sleep and more balance in her home/school life. Once her teachers began to understand the root cause of the problems, they dealt with her with more empathy and care. She responded by controlling her behaviour and finding a channel for her negative energy through sport (though, as I recall, netball became a contact sport for a while). What was so surprising to everyone involved was that as well as hiding her circumstances Karen was hiding a gentle, caring, committed side to her character that was well-developed. This was in sharp contrast to the aggression she showed her teachers and peers. She did not ever complain about having to do the most

➡

menial and inappropriate tasks at home yet at school she found it a struggle to remove her coat.

Students, like teachers, reveal different character traits at home and at school. In order to develop relationships with students it is often useful to try to blur the separation between the two. Try to find a less formal register within which to build your relationship; empathy is strength not weakness.

Why not try this?

Strategy selector: strategies for proactively developing relationships with students

Go through the checklist below checking off those strategies that you already use, selecting three ideas to adopt immediately and three to try over the next few weeks.

Strategies for proactively developing a relationship with a student	Already use	Use now	Use soon
Make a point of saying something positive as the student enters the classroom.			
Make a point of saying something positive as the student leaves the room.			
Identify colleagues who have positive relationships with the student and ask for advice.			
Give the student something they may be interested in – a newspaper article, webpage reference, loan copy of book.			
Channel your positive referrals through colleagues identified above to ensure your message has most impact.			

→

Strategies for proactively developing a relationship with a student	Already use	Use now	Use soon
Find specific areas of your work with the student to praise and encourage – 'Your design work is impressive; do you think you might have time to create some images for this display?'			
Have lunch at the same table/next to the student.			
Seek the student out at break duty for an informal conversation.			
Ask after the student's welfare, family, football team.			
Make a point of saying 'hello' when you pass them in the corridors.			
When the student makes good choices let other teachers know (loudly in the staffroom if you like).			
Balance your conversation with parents; start by giving positive feedback and then select just one or two areas of concern to discuss for immediate action.			
Phone home with good news about the student's behaviour.			
Get eye contact regularly with the student.			
Make it clear that you will only judge the student on their current behaviour; past reputation will not negatively influence your expectations.			
Respond to changes in their behaviour positively.			

→

Strategies for proactively developing a relationship with a student	Already use	Use now	Use soon
Give the student an appropriate responsibility in the classroom – distributing resources, drawing blinds, organising groups, etc.			
Make a point of marking work promptly with detailed feedback.			

Key ideas summary

Key idea	Benefit for the teacher	Benefit for the students
Challenging students are less likely to misbehave for teachers with whom they have developed a trusting relationship.	Students who previously disrupted classes and prevented learning are more willing to listen and follow the rules.	Students know that their teachers care enough to go the extra mile. They are unable to hide from the adult world.
Be proactive yet sensitive in slowly developing relationships with students who present challenging behaviours.	The teacher is realistic about the time needed to build a relationship and respectful of the student's right to privacy.	The teacher's approach is safe, unobtrusive and almost nonchalant.
Take advantage of the opportunities that visits/trips afford for building relationships.	Relationships are built through shared experience; conversations evolve more naturally outside the tensions of the institution.	Students learn more about their teachers and are able to interact with them in a less formal way.
Take care not to send mixed messages. Avoid delivering sanctions while trying to build your relationship.	The teacher holds the application of sanctions separate from informal conversations. The developing relationship is not abused.	The student understands that the teacher's high expectations of behaviour remain constant.
Follow agreed procedures for 'disclosure'.	The relationship is protected and confidentiality is not assumed.	The student is given clear information about the consequences of disclosing sensitive information.
Spending time with the students out of lessons in social areas affords you more time to develop positive relationships.	There are more opportunities for informal conversation; you get to know students without the pressures of the classroom.	Students are able to open up dialogues with their teachers that are not focused on class work.

107

Strategies for Primary, Secondary, FE and HE

Primary

'Parent on the shoulder' is a useful guide to check that your conversations with students are appropriate and the relationship is a professional one. Imagine that, regardless of the context in which you are in, your conversations can be overheard by the student's parent. With this level of self-awareness you will not go far wrong. More importantly, you will not go too far or divulge too much. Some students do not understand why there must be such boundaries, some are just excited to get to know you better, some deliberately try to overstep the mark and gain information in order to achieve an advantage. Revealing too much about your personal and social life may score some cool points, but can be easily misinterpreted and misreported. In an increasingly litigious society where child protection is uppermost in the minds of parents, you do not want to risk being misinterpreted.

Secondary, FE and HE

Questionnaires

Design a questionnaire for your students or ask students to create one for a partner using the sample questions below as a starting point. Students will often reveal far more in writing than they will in public conversation. You are not trying to pry into their private lives but to discover what motivates them, what are their passions and how you can make learning relevant to them.

Name one thing not many people know about you.	What is usually your first thought when you wake up?
Apple juice or orange juice?	What do you usually think about right before falling asleep?
Are you a morning or night person?	What's your favourite colour?
Which do you prefer, sweet or salty foods?	What's your favourite animal?
Ninjas or pirates?	Do you believe in extraterrestrials or life on other planets?
Are you a collector of anything?	Do you believe in ghosts?
If you could be any animal, what would you be?	Ever been addicted to a video/computer game? Which one(s)?
If you could have any superpower, what would it be?	→

You're given one million pounds, what do you spend it on?

Have any bad habits?

Which bad habits, if any, drive you crazy?

List three of your best personality traits.

List three of your worst personality traits.

Have any celebrity crushes?

List one thing you wish you could change about yourself.

What personality traits do you dislike in other people?

Are you mostly a clean or messy person?

If you could live anywhere in the world, where would you live?

If you could visit anywhere in the world, where would you go?

List five goals on your life's to-do list.

Name one regret you have.

What's your favourite song of the moment?

Name one thing you love about being a child.

What's your favourite song of all time?

What's your favourite thing to do on a Saturday night?

What's your favourite thing to do on a Sunday afternoon?

Have any hidden talents?

What would be your dream job?

If you could have three wishes granted, what would they be?

If you HAD to change your name, what would you change it to?

Do you believe in the afterlife?

Do you have brothers or sisters? If so, how many?

What is your favourite activity?

What is your least favourite activity?

What is your favourite school subject?

Have you been involved (or are you hoping to become involved) in any school activities – clubs, sports, etc.? If so, which ones?

What is your favourite type of music?

On the weekends I like to …

Someone I admire is … because …

If I could go anywhere for a day, I would go …

I learn the most when the teacher …

I learn the most when I …

I don't like it when teachers …

I don't like it when I'm asked to …

After school I will probably …

My ideal job would be …

When have you felt particularly successful in school?

When have you been the most proud of learning something?

What is the easiest part of school?

What is the hardest part of school?

What three things can I as the teacher do to help you become more successful as a student in this class?

What three things can you do as a student to help yourself be more successful this year?

Which is your favourite sports team?   What is your favourite movie?

Who is your favourite player?   Who is your favourite actor?

What is your favourite song?   What do you like to do for fun?

Who is your favourite artist?

30 days to make a change

Think about the changes that you would like to make in how you proactively build relationships. This might relate to an individual student, class or context. Commit to the new strategies for 30 days to allow them to embed into practice and your own teaching style.

In 30 days I will walk into work and ....

....

....

....

Make a commitment to try some of the strategies that have been suggested in this chapter.

My personal resolutions are:

1 _____   Review date _____

2 _____   Review date _____

3 _____   Review date _____

Building mutual trust with individuals and groups

'You can discover more about a person in an hour of play than in a year of conversation.'

(Plato)

The principle

Although achieving mutual trust between students and between teachers and students is a high expectation to set, it is not an unreachable ideal. A classroom that has mutual trust between learners is a place where risks can be taken and thoughts drafted aloud. Fear of public failure is reduced and higher-order thinking is more readily accessible for students. Creating mutual trust should not be an add-on to your behaviour management, but a core function of a successful classroom. In order to create an environment where trust can be nurtured there must be opportunities for students to: resolve conflict; complain when trust has been violated; and engage in learning activities where trust is given and received.

The practice

It is not really about respect but about trust. Before you are able to give respect you must give and receive trust. Defining trust for, and with, your students is an important first step. Students use a variety of terms for highlighting trust. Although their language might be different from yours, students' vocabulary has established definitions in their friendship groups and from home. Don't reject their definitions, but mix in your own ideas to write up or map out a collective definition of trust. Display it prominently. The way you act is critical. There are concrete actions that you can take to encourage mutual trust between learners. Try asking for regular student feedback on your teaching. You may choose to give a formal evaluation or engage in a series of less formal and more private conversations with students.

Give your students a real voice in how the teaching is received and build trust through a genuine dialogue about teaching and learning. Collect evidence by:

- Placing three labelled boxes at the door of the room and giving each student a token to place in the appropriate box to rate your teaching, how much they have learned or how much they enjoyed the lesson.
- Giving each student a card to plot how motivated they feel at five-minute intervals during the lesson.
- Interviewing students in small groups with agreed questions about how teaching and learning is organised in the classroom.

Make a point of refusing to allow students to lose face in public, regardless of their behaviour. If you encourage such loss of face overtly or covertly by ignoring the comments of other students, you are providing a poor model for your students. Avoid ridiculing students or using labels or derogatory nicknames and establish firm sanctions for students who name-call or put down others. There are many teachers who amuse themselves by allocating sarcastic and derogatory nicknames to their students. They may think that this is a way of connecting with their students or of injecting some humour into teaching, but in reality students can become confused about the sincerity of their teacher and quickly tire of being called 'Speedy', 'Clown' or 'Scruff'. Laugh with your students regularly, not at their expense and check your immediate response to students who make mistakes in public.

Detention v reparation

If you are issuing detentions where the responsibility is passed to someone else then consider changing detention for reparation. Effective sanctions are those which allow time for re-establishing expectations, re-chalking the boundary lines, repairing trust and making a commitment for the next lesson/day/10 minutes. Punitive sanctions satisfy the desire for mild revenge, separate the punishment from the original rule break and make students resentful.

Introducing reparation in a large north-London comprehensive meant individual teachers took responsibility each time a student reached the sanction. The initial impact of time on the workload of the individual was considerable but students quickly realised that this approach was going to be sustained and consistent. Students placed in reparation meet at a central point and are collected by teachers who can speak to them in the hall or move to a quieter space. The conversation is time-limited (15 minutes) and the focus clear. Students and teacher discuss the behaviour and not the student's identity. The discussion is structured to address what happened, reinforce expectations and reset behaviours for the next lesson. After some initial doubts the students saw the benefit of reparation over detention, relationships and mutual trust grew and the number of students reaching high-level sanctions reduced dramatically.

Lines (yes, they are still being used, widely), detentions that are not used to discuss behaviour, loss of time that is delegated to others, repeated sanctions that are subsumed into the schedule of the student's day (how many school children spend every lunchtime inside yet their behaviour is the same), humiliation and disproportionate sanctions ('Right, that is the second time I have asked you to sit down, go and wait outside the headteacher's office') don't set the right model or have a positive impact on behaviour.

There are principles that you can adopt and post up that help to define trust for both teachers and students:

Teachers	Students
Be consistent and predictable	Our words match our actions and we keep promises
Communicate accurately, openly and transparently	We talk through difficulties openly
Share and delegate control	If you give trust then you will receive it
Demonstrate empathy and understanding	Show concern for others
Perform competently	Do your best work, particularly when others are relying on you

In addition you can:

● Nurture a common identity for the class to create a sense of unity. In talk and actions use 'we' rather than 'me'.

- Give thought to the seating plan and use it to rotate students to work with each other, refining it so that you have variations on the seating plan for different activities.

- Establish or agree joint goals that are clearly defined, shared and displayed.

- Model and teach active listening: demonstrating appropriate verbal and physical language for a listener, modelling appropriate responses.

- Value work by displaying it and involving students in design and creation – perhaps a team of students who are trained in creating displays and touring the school at lunchtime to make repairs and replace displays.

Reflecting on practice

At Primary level, students' mutual trust is encouraged through sharing and delegating jobs in the classroom. A well-organised Year 5 teacher will have students handing out resources, clearing and cleaning the room, preparing areas for different activities, mounting display work, etc. The students learn how to share responsibility with others and accept responsibility for themselves. It is often said that Primary schools teach students to be independent and Secondary schools teach them not to be. Year 7 students in their new schools are often surprised when their responsibility for the classroom is removed, 'Right, I am counting out the scissors and I will come round and hand them out; don't touch them until I say so', and their freedom of movement restricted, 'Do not get out of your seat without written permission!' etc. The tasks and responsibilities that you are able to share may seem mundane and trivial but an ethos of shared responsibility is given a secure foundation.

When trust is violated it can have a negative effect on behaviour, performance and results. Trust violations stifle mutual support and need to be dealt with as soon as possible. As students develop their skills in reconciliation, you will need to take the lead in discussions on repair and reparation. Before you bring the two parties together, make sure that you have accurate written accounts or precise verbal reports. Insist on sincere, polite communication between the students and be prepared to reconvene the meeting if this cannot be achieved very quickly. Negotiate or provide students with clear choices on restitution and/or penance and help them to renegotiate their expectations for the future. Encourage students to reaffirm their commitment to building a trusting relationship.

Watch out for ...

- Ignoring violations of trust. By ignoring them you are risking a problem festering, growing and reemerging as a more complex conflict.

- Students who persistently violate trust and/or seem unable to give trust. These students will need additional support and their behaviour may be a sign of more complicated issues outside of the classroom.

Reflecting on practice

The kangaroo court of Judge Dix

Alistair was a highly intelligent student with quirky mannerisms and a slightly eccentric outlook. Other students were wary of him, he had no friends and was an outcast from the to-and-fro of social interaction. The rest of the students in the class were not challenging in their behaviour towards him but as a matter of course would disregard his views, laugh openly at him and tease him relentlessly, although not with intended malice. His status within the group was at an all-time low, his work was slipping from its high standard and it was clearly time for me to show some more public support.

Lessons with this group were good-humoured and amiable. We enjoyed our work, classes were rigorous and challenging and I felt comfortable taking risks. Over a period of time I instituted a system of reparation for 'crimes' committed by students over the course of the week. These were not behaviours that broke the rules or were connected directly with learning but were minor misdemeanours (often invented) that I would record and list, and then distribute related forfeits for during the last lesson on a Friday.

Taking Alistair aside one day I discussed the possibility of giving this evolving game a structure, a makeshift court with me as the judge and Alistair as my chief prosecution lawyer. It would, after all, help with some of our work on *To Kill a Mockingbird* and be most entertaining to boot. The following day he arrived complete with wig, gavel and a sign that must have taken him most of the evening to create. He adapted to his new role with aplomb, developing advanced 'legalese' and accurate speech structures for the courtroom.

We tried cases such as 'The Crown v Kirsty Appleton – the case of the broken pencil' or 'The Crown v Mark T – internet plagiarism or original thought?' There was never any real justice as I would always twist and subvert the verdict and summary sentence, and the students enjoyed this good-humoured 'kangaroo' justice. We had no end of volunteers to act as

→

the accused, defence lawyers, jury and witnesses for both sides. Everyone was keen to get involved and Alistair's performance improved week on week, while his status in the class grew alongside it. The other students began to understand what made him tick and were more willing to put their trust in him. They could see his skill and enthusiasm in action rather than hidden in his lengthy essays.

Slowly the teasing and laughing stopped and the other students began consulting him about impending cases, learning useful linguistic structures for their own speeches. They eventually (and quite rightly) convinced him to organise a *coup d'état*, placing me on trial at the end of the term and taking the judge's seat himself. The students had begun to understand Alistair and myself a little more: my trust in him had proved a good model for the class. They were prepared to trust him a little more and give more time and effort to understand him.

Why not try this?

Trust exercises sit comfortably alongside long-established frameworks for trust-building, such as 'circle time'. They are used in the theatre to quickly establish mutual physical trust between actors. These exercises:

- Immediately identify barriers to giving and receiving trust
- Actively involve students in using strategies to promote trust
- Throw up questions and ideas about self-discipline
- Encourage students who rarely work together to build trust
- Highlight students who have difficulty giving and receiving trust on a one-to-one basis
- Are fun, thoroughly enjoyable and rewarding.

When I am leading a session on trust it is always made clear to the students that if they do not follow the rituals they will be asked to sit out immediately (and later reintegrated) as the safety of students is the highest priority. Establish your learning ritual early and implement it vigorously. When the atmosphere in the room is really focused, the exercises are tense, exciting and revealing. It is a good idea to start with the first activity and build up in small steps, perhaps using each one as a rung on a 'ladder of trust'.

Some of the activities outlined below can be run in a classroom, others need more space. There are more advanced trust exercises, such as 'falling' and 'leaping into a sea of arms', but they need to be explained physically rather than read

→

and interpreted. The origins of these exercises can be found in Clive Barker's *Theatre Games* (1977).

Initiate a 'stop' signal for the whole group and between students. Try a shortened countdown in case you want to stop them quickly and encourage students to use their partner's name as well as 'Stop', e.g., use 'Ewan, stop' to differentiate commands from pairs working nearby.

1   **Leading the blind**

In pairs, A and B, students lead each other using a tie or piece of string. A holds the string in both hands with eyes tightly shut while B slowly leads him around the room, avoiding contact with the rest of the participants. As are attempting to give trust by keeping their eyes open and Bs are receiving trust and trying to use it responsibly. Experiment with shorter and longer leashes, leading around objects and, in controlled conditions, over obstacles.

2   **Trust cars**

Again in pairs, A with eyes shut and B leading, but this time from behind – A is the 'car' and B the 'driver'. To begin with there are three agreed signals: hand on the left shoulder turn left (and keep turning until the hand is removed), hand on the right shoulder turn right, and flat hand placed (gently!) between the shoulder blades to stop. As the exercise develops students will naturally develop other ideas for useful controls. B 'drives' A around the room; trust is seen to be broken if A opens his eyes.

3   **Walking into walls**

A and B stand opposite each other seven or eight metres apart. With eyes closed, A will walk towards B and only stop when the command is given. If the command is late, or A walks too fast the two will collide. Practise the exercise to show how long it takes for the command to be registered and the walker halted. Extend this exercise for responsible students so that the walker speeds up or is heading towards the wall rather than his partner.

Weave in some key questions for students to discuss in preparation for the exercises or as reflection:

● How do we give trust?

● How do you receive trust?

● What stops trust-building?

● What helps you give and receive trust?

● What can you do to encourage trust?

● What kinds of trust do we need in the classroom?

Key ideas summary

Key idea	Benefit for the teacher	Benefit for the students
Map a collective definition of trust with your students.	A common language and understanding is used in the classroom; the display is useful to refer to.	Student language and definition of ideas is given status.
Do not allow students to be ridiculed publicly.	You can remain impartial and fair.	The learning space is free from humiliation, the teacher can be trusted to provide support when necessary.
Nurture a common identity with the class; identify shared goals.	Responsibility for learning and target-setting is shared. High expectations are defined and sustained.	Students have a responsibility to each other and a voice in defining a shared vision.
Laugh with your students and not at them.	The teacher does not casually risk damaging a relationship with any student.	Students understand that their teacher has a sense of humour, not just a cruel streak.
Establish a simple procedure for repairing violations of trust.	Incidents are dealt with calmly and efficiently; conflicts between students or between teacher and student are not allowed to grow.	Students have responsibility for repairing and maintaining trust.
Share responsibility for learning and organising the classroom with students.	The teacher has more time to dedicate to students. The learning space is more efficiently organised.	Students learn to manage their own learning independently and responsibly. They feel that they are trusted.

Strategies for Primary, Secondary, FE and HE

Primary

Rotate roles and responsibilities. Give formal titles to roles and use badges, hats and costume to encourage enjoyment in responsibility.

Secondary

What strategies work with mixed age or 'vertical' tutor groups?

Deep sense of belonging:

- Playing and laughing together
- Regular trips out of school
- Ownership of the environment – creating displays together
- Competition with other groups
- Tutor group online forum
- Negotiated and contracted agreements over conduct, displayed and referred to incessantly
- Daily/weekly rituals that everyone shares.

Personal relationships:

- Insisting all members of the tutor group greet each other around the site.

Peer mentoring:

- Giving older students responsibility; associate tutors, learning advisors, advocacy.

Purposeful conversation:

- Paired reading
- Debating local and wider political issues
- Equal voting rights
- Routines that allow each student a voice.

Democratic group:

- Student voice
- Rotating responsibilities
- Insisting that students of all ages lead.

FE and HE

Autonomy, choice and independence over learning is hugely motivating and builds trust. Students who are machine gunned with targets, levels, objectives and outcomes sense that they are not learners with any control. They sense that they cannot be trusted to take responsibility for their own learning. Targets that fall from above in the adult world are rarely embraced with enthusiasm. So it goes with students. Students who set their own targets, take responsibility for their own learning, contribute to displays, have a role with the group tend to be engaged in the fabric of learning. They are motivated at a deeper level. Those who are 'PowerPointed' into submission or constantly medicated with computers build an addiction to the screen but are not trusted to learn independently. Their motivation is on the surface, 'Ooooo flickery screen!', and they are occupied, but the learning is not satisfying and the information gleaned does not embed itself in the memory.

30 days to make a change

Think about the changes that you would like to make in how you build trust with students. This might relate to an individual student, class or context. Commit to the new strategies for 30 days to allow them to embed into practice and your own teaching style.

In 30 days I will walk into work and ....

....

....

....

....

Make a commitment to try some of the strategies that have been suggested in this chapter.

My personal resolutions are:

1 _____ Review date _____

2 _____ Review date _____

3 _____ Review date _____

Students with extreme behaviour and behaviour-changing conditions

'I see myself as a roving mosquito, choosing its target.'

(Kenneth Williams)

The principle

You can't improve the behaviour of the hard to reach by throwing behaviour-management techniques at them or by condemning them with years of punishment and exclusion. You can't change their behaviour, attitude or anger with magic behaviour dust. Neither can you address what motivates them to disengage or interrupt years of learned behaviour overnight. Change with the most challenging pupils does not run in straight lines. There are many cul-de-sacs on the way to the straight and narrow. You need to be patient, kind and determined not to give up on any of your students. You are the adult and you need to keep a clear perspective even when these students try to reject your help.

Some students have such complex needs that senior colleagues and external agencies will have an input, but it is unrealistic to expect them to have an immediate impact. Even students with the most extreme emotional and behavioural difficulties can and do succeed. To have a chance of succeeding with students experiencing difficulty controlling their behaviour you will need to invest time in your relationship with them and accept that this investment is for the long term.

The practice

Managing the behaviour of students who will happily step over each and every boundary with abandon takes time, dedication and a degree of stubbornness on your part. Alongside the daily firefight you need the drip feed of a more strategic plan to address the heart of the problem. Hooking the hard to reach requires the patience and guile of a master fisherman and the heart of a lion tamer.

There is a moment in all of our lives when we realise that the adult world is not as dependable, safe and secure as we once believed. For the majority of young people this realisation comes in the teenage years, for a lucky few their awakening is delayed further, while for many many others it came during the Primary school years. When a parent who promises that they will be there for you suddenly isn't it can be the catalyst for even young children to distrust the adult world. Trust issues at home can be compounded by high staff turnover at school or through too many well-meaning people trying to give short-term help. Put simply, children who are 'hard to reach' may have decided that adults should be given a wide berth. The barriers come up. Some try to disengage with learning, some stop communicating, most demonstrate their anger, confusion and lack of trust with behaviour that says 'leave me alone, I am not worth bothering with'.

> 'Just under 50% of children in care had reached the national curriculum test level expected for their age compared to 82% of all children.'
>
> (Department for Children, Schools and Families, April 2008)

The drip feed of your relentlessly positive and nurturing dialogue is the foundation of a long-term strategy. Directly challenge students' negative assumptions about their own ability, 'You are not an idiot because you have the wrong answer', and persistently suggest alternative thoughts, such as, 'Spelling aside, this is a beautiful sentence' or, 'You have a real talent for choosing the right combination of words.' Over time the waves of positive thought begin to erode the barriers to their potential. Continually attack their assumption that you are going to be like the other adults that have let them down in the past, 'I care about you, I am here to help you and I am not going away.' Use examples of their previous appropriate behaviour to hook your judgements about their character, 'Do you remember, yesterday, when you helped me clear up the room? That is the kind of behaviour I want to see today, that is the person I know and trust.'

With those foundations in place you can start fishing. Find what talent or ability has been smuggled in with the obvious emotional baggage and build on it. If it is too well hidden, consider putting the hook in yourself. There are times when many of us need to be led rather than constantly be given choices. For children who are floating around aimlessly you may need to convince them that you have found a bait they like rather than wait for them to choose one they like. Once you have them interested in the bait, make sure that you have other members of staff/ parents/significant adults to act as 'convincers', reinforcing this new aptitude. Plan for all of your hard work to be thrown back in your face, more than once. Plan to invest your time for no immediate reward.

In amongst the chaos of the day to day, be mindful of the present moment. You are doing something remarkable, something altruistic, something life changing. Altaf may not thank you immediately for having a profoundly positive impact on his life, but then teaching was never about what I can get for myself but about what I can do for others.

TOP TIP!

As a class teacher you are able to instigate a 'Class Report' to monitor the behaviour of individuals who are causing concern. This can be particularly useful to monitor students who display sequences of inappropriate behaviour in your lessons. The fact that the report is sent up the internal chain and also sent home gives it weight. You will often find that it only takes a few bad lessons for the student to realise that a sheet of paper with incidents recorded and dated is not going to go down well with its intended audience. Typically, students strive to improve their choices to balance the initially negative behaviour. Your regular conversations with the student will also give you the opportunity to focus on positive changes and reinforce them strongly. Use the template on www. pearsoned.co.uk/essentialguides to design your own 'Class Report' form.

Fairness

It would be very easy to declare that everyone, regardless of their individual needs, must follow the same rules in your classroom. Yet working with students who have social, emotional and behavioural difficulties (SEBD) is not that linear. It requires a more flexible approach. Everybody needs to accept that at different times you will make decisions that may not appear fair but are in the best interests of individuals.

Fairness does not always mean perfect equality between the students. Very often more challenging students will be working with a team of people in the school and from external frontline support services. There may be many different people negotiating or setting behaviour targets: their parents, tutor, senior member of staff, specialist behaviour teacher, social worker, probation officer, counsellor, etc. With everyone working in the best interests of the student the support ought to have benefits over the medium and long term. In the short term and at the class level it is very difficult for professionals who are not present to have an immediate influence on behaviour.

Pastoral leaders who have a high level of input with a challenging student will often encounter them, report card in hand, being escorted down the corridor after engaging in precisely the behaviours they have spent two days discussing. The teacher is distraught as it seems that even the middle management and external agencies are having no effect. For students who have difficulty managing their behaviour the process of change can be slow and frustrating. You need to do everything you can to collaborate and encourage change.

At a class level the visible impact of additional support may be the student wafting their report card in your face. The report will have pre-agreed targets, rules and, for some students, procedures to follow for removing them from the lesson.

Don't be tempted to undermine the work of others by doing any of the following:

> Use the report as a negotiating tool with the student to try to bribe them into behaving appropriately: 'If you stop hitting Clive I will give you a good report.'
>
> Allow the student to negotiate their way into a good report after a lesson where they didn't follow the rules or achieve their targets, 'Aw, go on, sir, give me a tick for that one, I was really good this lesson. Please, sir, Arsenal won, you must be in good mood.' (They are very good at it and know that it works.)
>
> Try to avoid confrontation with the student by giving them a good report. There are some students who will fly into a rage or descend into tears when they see what you have recorded on their reports. Their reaction, however extreme, should not influence your judgement on whether they have met their targets.
>
> Write anything on the report that is a judgement on the student: 'Still can't behave, rude boy.'
>
> Leave reports where they can be read by other students.

In some circumstances it is preferable to return the report card to the student as they are on the way out of the lesson, having filled it in already. This can help to avoid confrontation as the students read the outcome. The reason that report cards can be such a flashpoint is that the student has sanctions hanging over them that they would much rather avoid. They may have sanctions linked between home and school that affect their social time, access to media or income. The fact that they are worried about their sanctions is a good thing and might just be enough to move some students away from the edge. By fulfilling your responsibilities at the class level you are making it clear to the student that their destiny is in their own hands. Try:

Reinforcing the ritual for the report card to be given to the teacher.

Giving sincere praise and encouragement for students who follow the rules and achieve targets.

Showing concern if you see from the card that the student is having a bad day.

Reminding students on their reports that every good lesson stands out and counts in their favour.

Making time for students, be it in tutor/form group, around the school or at an appropriate time in the lesson, for those who are keen to show and discuss their report with you.

Although I recognise that report card systems are not a universal solution, they do provide valuable information for monitoring behaviour across the curriculum and build a framework for discussion and targeting intervention. Many students find the process allows them a chance to reflect on their behaviour; some will ask to be 'put on report', others will use the report card blank to evaluate their own behaviour.

I can't teach this student – it's not fair on the rest of the class

We have all heard this, and some have said it more than once, but it is worth considering what happens when we give up on a student and begin the process of excluding them from education. I know we enter a wider political realm here, but it starts in individual classrooms.

The situation is not uncommon. The behaviour of an individual pupil is extreme and disruptive to the rest of the learning. The student's needs appear to be so complex you begin to question why they are not accommodated elsewhere. You have tried and failed to manage the behaviour, and you have watched as colleagues have tried to intervene and provide support but appear to be making little impact. Exasperated, you demand that the student is excluded from your class. He is duly removed; you breathe a heavy sigh of relief and feel that your actions are in the best interest of the majority of the students. For the short term, they may be.

→

A student who is repeatedly excluded is likely to be in a cycle of negative behaviour:

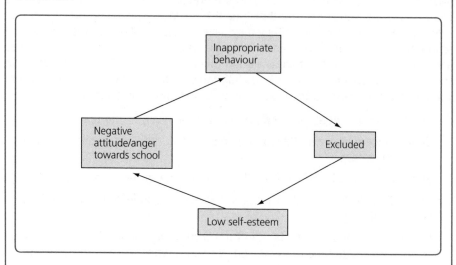

By excluding the student you are allowing the cycle to continue. There is certainly a small minority of students who cannot fit into mainstream education and it is right that they should be given opportunities to be educated elsewhere. There is a more significant number who are simply moved around different institutions. These students learn fairly quickly that adults cannot always be relied on to support them. Many students with emotional and behavioural difficulties know this already from home. Adults who have shown commitment to them in the past can leave suddenly. In schools and colleges their distrust of adults is reconfirmed by teachers who give up on them. The message they can infer from both sides is that there is something wrong with them.

As a teacher you are responsible for all of the students within your care, regardless of their individual needs. Don't give up on any individual and tell them so. You may need to exclude students as part of higher-level sanctions, but this should always be temporary and you will need to commit time outside of the classroom to providing additional support. Phone and visit parents, stay after school, arrange for extra support in lessons from outside agencies, and be proactive in developing a trusting relationship with the student.

Successful teachers go the extra mile not just because they care about the individual who is experiencing difficulties but also because of the rest of the class. They send a clear message that their job is to ensure everyone succeeds and that as a class everyone has a responsibility to support each other. In the classroom, as in life, there will be people who at different times find it hard to fit in. Rather than rejecting these people we need to show them care, compassion and respect. Part of your role as a teacher is to model this, demonstrating to your students an inclusive approach to learning together.

Pivotal moments in managing challenging behaviour

- Heightened self-awareness, deliberate choice in approach/language/tone.
- Disconnect their behaviour from their identity.
- Separate their behaviour from your emotion.
- Find the hook or convince the pupil you have found one.
- Shift behaviours to the past tense as soon as possible.
- Quell the first signs of confrontation by reminding the pupil of a moment when they behaved appropriately.
- Using presupposition to challenge limiting self-belief and negative internal monologues.
- Scripted, predictable, emotionless responses for pupils who try to divert, escalate or push your buttons.
- Playing the longer game with an eye to the strategic outcomes.
- Refuse to accept the labels that the child has been given.
- Intensively and overtly model appropriate behaviour.
- Actively build mutual trust and an appropriate professional relationship.
- Address the pupil's internal voice.
- Build and maintain a strong relationship with the home.
- Direct support to address external issues affecting behaviour.

There will be times when many of the students will need additional support in managing their behaviour. Your sole focus cannot always be the majority of students; in that majority there are students who may not need extra attention today but will do tomorrow. Aim to try to break or at least slow down the cycles of negative behaviour. Saying 'I can't teach this child' says more about your commitment to your students than it does about behaviour that is difficult to manage.

Which steps have you taken to address and improve the behaviour of the student?

- Adapted, individualised and negotiated rules, rewards and sanctions.
- Set short-term targets that are reinforced by praise, acknowledgement and reward.
- Consistently and calmly applied sanctions.
- Made a detailed record of behaviour over the course of eight lessons.
- Initiated face-to-face discussion with parents with the support of senior staff.
- Drawn up a behaviour contract/agreement with everyone concerned having an input (see www.pearsoned.co.uk/essentialguides).
- Agreed mechanism with the student to indicate when they need 'time out' (see www.pearsoned.co.uk/essentialguides).
- Altered seating plan.
- Agreed strategies with teaching assistant or other adults working in the classroom.
- Kept praise, reward and sanctions discreet and private.
- Used modelling to reflect behaviour back to the student and help them to gain a better perspective on their actions.
- Sought guidance from senior or key colleagues.
- Referred to appropriate internal channels and chased these referrals.
- Provided information and support to encourage the input of external agencies.
- Gone out of my way to invest time and energy into building a relationship with the student.
- Considered carefully whether the student is part of a small minority which needs specialist schooling or whether he is part of the larger group of students that can be included in mainstream education.

Your seating plan is crucial when you teach students who exhibit extreme behaviours. Make sure that you seat them in a place that you always return to, and away from their regular audience. You might find it useful to speak privately to the students that do sit nearby about how they can best support others while sustaining their own focus. Keep gently reminding them about the routine that you expect from them, and if you move from seated work to active work, introduce the new routine with care. Get the student to repeat the instructions back to you so you are sure they have a clear understanding. Don't be surprised if you have to refocus the student during the task: this might be a quick intervention where you take them back to the agreed learning ritual or a more private conversation away from the class.

Your targets for these students need to be short-term ones. Providing a target for the end of the next lesson may be appropriate for students who are in control of their behaviour, but for challenging students it may be necessary to set a target only for the next five minutes of work. You will also need to explain your expectations and targets for their social conduct alongside this. Do not assume that they know how to work in groups or even individually. If you are trying to break a negative pattern of behaviour it is important that your starting point is that they don't know how to behave appropriately. Just as early-years teachers know it is their responsibility to teach the children social skills and empathy, so with challenging students you must build this into your teaching style.

Match your short-term targets with short-term praise and rewards that can be agreed with the student. It is important to realise that students with a negative label don't often attract regular praise and rewards. They are more likely to be closely observed for inappropriate behaviour and you need to change this focus. I'm not suggesting that you heap rewards on challenging students, it is your verbal praise and acknowledgement that is most important, but if you set a five-minute target and the student reaches this or makes strong moves towards it then it must be immediately reinforced if the level of work is to be sustained. Do it privately and discreetly; use eye contact, non-verbal cues and written comments to let the student know that their behaviour is appreciated and valued. Be prepared for your responses to be rejected and even thrown back in your face. If you really want to break the cycle it will take patience and commitment. Make your classroom a place where they can succeed, a place where the teacher is utterly consistent and the seeds of trust will be allowed to grow.

TOP TIP!

When incidents occur, and they will, your response to them is crucial. Teach students who choose to engage in more extreme behaviours a simple principle: when they challenge and confront they don't get your emotional response; when they behave appropriately they get your positive emotion, passion and enthusiasm. Make your interventions to challenging behaviour emotionless, robotic, dull, repetitive, predictable and safe. Save your emotion for when it is most needed and has most impact. Break the connection between their inappropriate behaviour and your negative emotion. Many students have learnt that extreme behaviour results in dramatic responses from the teacher. They may have slipped into negative behaviour patterns because they enjoy these reactions. If you want to break the cycle, your responses should be carefully measured, even in the most challenging situations. With your emotional brain carefully in check, and verbal and physical language controlled, calmly go through the same script. You may find it useful to use the sample structure for intervention (in Chapter 7) or a simplified version of this.

Intervention scripts that protect everyone

1st warning (verbal)

I saw/heard you chose to ... You broke rule number ...
This is a verbal warning.
You now have the chance to make intelligent choices.
Thank you for listening.

2nd warning (written)

I saw/heard you chose to ... You broke rule number ...
This is a written warning.
Think carefully about your next move; you are in charge of your behaviour and can make intelligent choices.
Thank you for listening.

3rd warning – one minute after

I saw/heard you chose to ... You broke rule number ...
This is the third time I have spoken to you. You have chosen to speak to me for a minute after the lesson.
.... (student's name), do you remember when ....
(model of previous good behaviour)? That is the standard of behaviour I expect from you.
If you choose to break the rules again you leave me no choice but to ask you to leave the room.
Think very carefully about your next move, I know that you can make intelligent choices.
Thank you for listening.

4th warning – asked to leave the room

I saw/heard you choose to ... You have broken rule number ...
You need to leave the room, I will come and speak to you in a moment/five minutes/at lunchtime.

Reflecting on practice

Here is an example of a staged, scripted approach in action. SEBD School in Sussex caters for students with severe social, emotional and behavioural difficulties. In 2007 the school was in crisis: HMI inspectors said it was failing and needed radical change. Teachers lacked the expertise to deal with students' behaviour, and there was no consistent response to rule-breaking. Aggressive and even violent confrontations between teachers and pupils occurred on a daily basis.

Ofsted demanded that pupil behaviour improve, the number of exclusions be reduced and the school as a whole become a safer and calmer environment for learning.

I had two months to train all the staff in practical behaviour management, create a school-wide system of rewards and sanctions, repair the broken trust between staff and students, and finally to help the school to come out of 'Special Measures' status.

The head wanted all the adults in the school to respond to bad behaviour with precise, scripted responses. This was a radical and risky approach and I had to design an innovative training programme to make it work. Using various active learning techniques, I helped the staff to create and rehearse their own scripts. The training included intensive improvisation exercises as trainees had to become experts at deflecting student protests.

The results have been remarkable. Ofsted has taken the school out of Special Measures and, unusually, mentioned the trainers in their report: 'The Pivotal Eduation programme has had a significant impact on improving pupil/staff interactions and in establishing a calmer school,' it said. 'The students confirm that they like the new system because it is transparent, fair, all staff know the procedures and less time is wasted in lessons. They know exactly what to expect when they misbehave.'

Surveys conducted by the school revealed that, 'All students said that they now learn in lessons, get the help they need and are consistently rewarded for good work', and that, 'All parents believe that the school promotes and expects good behaviour.'

The Head of the School, said, 'The impact of these strategies led to a much calmer atmosphere in the school, teachers more confident with dealing with behaviour, a positive impact on teaching and learning and, because out-of-class figures were reduced, progress in achievement was judged by Ofsted to be good with elements of outstanding.'

TOP TIP!

Some students have difficulty in controlling their anger and/or frustration, but can recognise when they are about to lose it. With these students you may find it useful to use a 'time out' card. The card is held by the student and placed on the teacher's desk when they need to leave the room to calm down. You will need to set a limit to the amount of times the student can use this in a single lesson. With some students it may be necessary to connect the use of the card with the requirement to complete a think sheet (see www.pearsoned.co.uk/essentialguides) to allow them to reflect on what brought them to this point. This will encourage students not to overuse it and allow you to reflect with them and plan for the next lesson.

Let other teachers, parents and external agencies know when that student decides to follow the rules. Record your comments on paper as verbal feedback can be lost. There will inevitably be detailed documentation on their crimes and problems; you have a responsibility to record their positive behaviour with as much care.

Modelling and 'holding up the mirror'

A colleague and friend tells of a student who responded to even the simplest request with the exaggerated grunts, sighs and flinches that we most associate now with Harry Enfield's or Catherine Tate's teenage characters. She became exasperated with his behaviour and decided to tackle it head-on.

Holding the student behind during the lunch hour, and in private, she sought the support of a colleague and asked the student if he minded watching while she demonstrated the behaviour that she was observing from him. He agreed and she mimicked, fairly accurately, a typical response to a straightforward request. 'Could I have a look at your work please?', 'What! (sighs), oh God (exhales loudly, tutting, more sighing, etc.), get out of my face, etc.' At the end of her demonstration the boy was ashen-faced. He was shocked at the reflection of his own behaviour and felt embarrassed that other students had seen him behave in this way. In an instant he resolved to check his behaviour with more care.

Many of us would assume that he was aware of his original behaviour pattern and engaging in it deliberately. It was the clarity of the teacher's judgement and her careful and sensitive use of modelling that turned the situation round. She was able to hold up the mirror to his behaviour and allow him to accept this information in a controlled environment.

Younger students need this mirror as they find it difficult to externalise their own behaviour. The 4-year-old who pleads repeatedly to be allowed to go first only sees the situation from his own viewpoint. Encouraging him to see his behaviour from the outside allows him to begin understanding the impact it has on others. When you see 15-year-olds engaging in the same selfish behaviour of a 4-year-old, it might be that they too need to be taught empathy.

Watch out for ...

- Making assumptions about a student's behaviour because of their label or from what you have heard about them in the staffroom. SEBD students rarely get the opportunity to have a clean sheet and can feel the weight of their label/reputation pulling them into a negative pattern. There is nothing more soul-destroying for a student who is trying to find a way of changing people's attitudes towards them than to find that new people they meet have already made up their minds.

- Getting frustrated because the student does not appear to be modifying their disruptive behaviour patterns. Regardless of your level of skill, you are not going to turn them round in an instant. Set your targets for improving their behaviour in the longer term: think about months and years, instead of days and weeks.

- Contacting home without first checking with the appropriate member of staff. It is likely that the institution will already have identified the most effective communication with home. This will be carefully planned and regular. Picking up the phone or making unauthorised contact may trample on the work of other professionals. You also need to think about what the consequences for the child may be at home. There may be very good reasons why senior staff are the point of contact within the school.

- Assuming inappropriate behaviour is directed at you. The student who swears in frustration because he doesn't understand how to engage in the work is not swearing directly at you. Although you may not agree with the student's choice of language or choice of behaviour, you need to accept that their reactions may not be the same as that of other students. Whilst you should not ignore inappropriate behaviour, measure and differentiate your response to it.

Asperger's syndrome and autism

Asperger's syndrome is variant of autism. Young people with Asperger's present different individual variations of the condition. Although this guidance may help you to understand some of the key issues and practical strategies, you will need to get to know the student well and adapt ideas accordingly. Asperger's is predominantly a male condition (9:1 male/female). Lorna Wing (Burgoine and Wing, 1983) described the main clinical features of Asperger's syndrome as:

● Lack of empathy
● Naïve, inappropriate, one-sided interaction
● Little or no ability to form friendships
● Pedantic, repetitive speech
● Poor non-verbal communication
● Intense absorption in certain subjects
● Clumsy and ill-coordinated movements and odd postures.

Those who are diagnosed with Asperger's syndrome, autism (ASD), and to some extent ADHD (attention deficit hyperactivity disorder), view or interpret the world very differently. As a teacher you need to understand how their condition affects their perception. There are practical strategies you can adopt; they must be adjusted for the individual, implemented with empathy and have the flexibility to be adapted for different contexts. The strategies that you use for managing the behaviour of other students are still relevant here, with certain aspects given more emphasis:

● Maintain consistency and predictability – of lesson structure, intervention, response.
● The adult's emotional control – don't take it personally even if the student appears to be rude, making comments such as 'You are fat'. Their frankness may be the result of their literal world.
● Planned and controlled use of language (verbal, tonal and physical) – avoid sarcasm, over exaggeration, imagery. Communication should be precise as it may be interpreted literally. 'I am going to explode!' may mean exactly that to the autistic student.
● Modelling appropriate behaviour and basic routines/rules. Model for and with other students to show them how to communicate effectively. Model for the student with the condition to show them precisely the behaviours that you want.
● Encouraging positive friendships and helping the student to make and sustain positive relationships with others.

- Using time out to release tension. Accepting that at times the control they exert over their behaviour may have built up tension that needs to be released.
- Consistently apply routines, rules and rituals – in a visual (signs, symbols and language) form, and as praise and sanctions.
- Use visual cues, visual support for learning.
- Control the physical environment – size and division of space, level and range of noise (particularly unexpected noise).
- Prepare students for changes to the normal routine.

Why not try this?

- Prepare for the student's arrival by inviting them to come to the classroom, look at where they will sit, the equipment they will use and the environment in which they will work. Negotiate with the student, ask questions, rehearse the arrival of the whole group and examine common classroom routines.

- Take care over transitions between activities – prepare the student for the transition in good time, establish rituals for transitions, map the transition as a visual routine on the wall, perhaps using photographs of the students.

- Have a clear visual plan of the lesson in the same place for the student to look at when s/he enters. Break the lesson down into chunks and use symbols or photographs so that they know what to expect: e.g., 1. Sitting and listening; 2. Writing; 3. Group discussion; 4. Fire alarm, etc.

- Explain the sequence of a complex task. You might prepare for the arrival of the student by using the other students to model the routines on video or as a series of photographs.

- Apply rewards and consequences calmly using tickets/Post-its/pictures. Consider giving the student a mechanism to record where they are on the sanctions/rewards ladder throughout the lesson.

- Make a series of flashcards with clear symbols to show to the student if they are interrupting or shouting out at inappropriate times. Use a keyring to hold the cards and easily flip from one to the next.

- Give the student a 'time out' card that they can leave on your desk if they need to leave the room and release some tension. The card might say, 'I need to leave the room now, I am not being rude, I just need to take 5'. Again, this card could be designed with symbols or using a photograph.

- Be aware of students misinterpreting body language, tone of voice, facial expressions, gestures, intent.

→

- Use a picture dictionary to introduce new vocabulary, support learning with concrete materials.

- When necessary, reduce your language to key words or cues to emphasise the main message you are trying to convey.

- Often a student with ASD will read fluently and with ease and yet may not have comprehended what has been read. Check for understanding, help the student to bridge the gaps in comprehension, and give them extra time to re-read when necessary.

- Carefully choose students for group and paired activities. Re-run the routines for turn taking and sharing responsibility during the task.

- Use the other students as models for appropriate behaviour. Ask the student to observe the others and copy what they are doing.

- Encourage friendships working with all students to help them understand a little more and judge a little less.

- Take care when planning activities. Consider avoiding loud noises and unexpected attacks on the senses: loud noises, boisterous groups, sudden interruptions, sudden movement.

TOP TIP!

A key feature of autism is the inability to generalise information from one context to another. For example, a student learns to write his name with a blue pencil with Mrs Hussain. When the same task is presented with a green pencil the student does not recognise this pencil as the same 'tool' with the same function. Similarly, if the task is re-presented by Mr Knowles with different language the student considers this to be a new and different task. Skills are not generalised. It helps the student when adults generalise the familiar by looking at different pencils, shapes, sizes, with and without rubbers and defining what makes a pencil a pencil.

Drugs, nutrition, behaviour disorders, TV and new media

There are many issues that teachers have no direct influence on but which affect the management of behaviour. Students who have been diagnosed with ADHD or other emotional or behavioural disorders, students prescribed Ritalin, students who are malnourished, exhausted through lack of sleep, experimenting with controlled drugs or troubled by a complicated domestic situation, present themselves in the classroom and their behaviour needs to be managed. It is important that you are as informed as possible about the external factors that directly affect behaviour in the classroom. Your knowledge and understanding of the key issues may be useful when you are asked for advice by parents and you will be able to take best advantage of opportunities to have a positive influence.

ADHD (attention deficit hyperactivity disorder)

There is much conflicting evidence about ADHD. Critics argue that it is a convenient label that gives a medical reason for poor behaviour; others point to the use of brain-imaging techniques which demonstrate that it has a biological basis. ADHD, which is also known as attention deficit disorder (or ADD), hyperkinetic child syndrome, minimal brain damage, minimal brain dysfunction in children, minimal cerebral dysfunction and psycho-organic syndrome in children, is a remarkably non-specific disorder. The symptoms which characterise the disorder may include: a chronic history of a short attention span, distractibility, impulsivity and moderate to severe hyperactivity. Learning may or may not be impaired.

There is certainly little consistency in diagnosis, and moving between schools it is not unusual to find students with the same label demonstrating few similar symptoms or even similar behaviours. The truth is that some parents will push for a diagnosis of ADHD in search of reason for a temporary period of poor behaviour, and some overworked doctors will submit to it too easily. However, this does not negate the accurate and extremely worrying diagnosis for students who genuinely have a long-term medical condition. The treatment for ADHD will, in part, necessitate a behavioural approach with home, school and external support agencies working in partnership. The other part of the treatment brings together a range of key issues that surround ADHD.

Prescription drugs

When a child has been given a medical label it is possible to offer a treatment. With Western medicine it is usually a drug which is profit-linked. The amphet-amine-based drug Ritalin is widely used to counter the behavioural symptoms of ADHD and its use is extremely controversial.

Latest figures showed that GPs wrote more than 535,000 prescriptions for anti-hyperactivity drugs in 2007 – more than 10,000 a week. The figure has doubled since 2002 (Donnelly, 2008).

These figures are shocking and probably don't reflect the true number of students taking medication. If you count parents who are bypassing their GP and buying them on the Internet, 'without prescription, by credit card, by overnight courier', and students who are buying them to aid intensive periods of study, the figures are bound to rise. This is in the context of rapidly increasing recorded prescriptions.

Children as young as three, whose brains are still developing, are being prescribed mind-altering drugs. In America there are documented cases of children as young as 15 months being prescribed Ritalin. Yet many doctors are concerned that Ritalin is being wrongly prescribed and used as a sticking plaster for a period of poor behaviour.

Peter R. Breggin MD, Director of the International Center for the Study of Psychiatry and Psychology and associate faculty member at The Johns Hopkins University, said: 'Ritalin does not correct biochemical imbalances – it causes them.'

A child taking Ritalin might have more focused behaviour, but although that might mean less disruption in the classroom, does it really help the child? And should we give a child a powerful and potentially hazardous drug just because it keeps him quiet?

When children are prescribed strong medication it must be a cause of grave concern to everyone; when it is on this scale the search for preventive and alternative treatment takes on more urgency.

> 'In school-age children and young people with severe ADHD, drug treatment should be offered as the first-line treatment. Parents should also be offered a group-based parent-training/education programme.'
>
> (National Institute for Health and Clinical Excellence (NICE), Attention deficit hyperactivity disorder, NHS Clinical Guidelines CG72, http://guidance.nice.org.uk/CG72, September 2008)

Controlled drugs

If you suspect that students are under the influence of controlled drugs (including alcohol) whilst in school, try to gather evidence rather than jumping in with accusations. Whether you are right or not you are unlikely to improve the situation by publicly declaring your judgement. Deal with the student's immediate behaviour professionally whilst subtly seeking a second opinion from a colleague. You can then report and discuss your observations to a senior colleague. A sizeable minority of students will always want to experiment with controlled substances; your responsibility is to reinforce the policy of no drugs in school, open clear pathways for students to seek advice and guidance whilst maintaining positive relationships. If experimentation develops into a regular habit it is those with the most developed relationships that are likely to have most influence on the student.

Nutrition

There are alternatives to quick-fix drugs for students who are diagnosed with or demonstrate symptoms of ADHD. The evidence of a link between nutrition and behaviour is compelling. Teachers have always been able to recognise students who arrive at school without a proper breakfast. From slipping a hungry child an apple, to free milk and breakfast clubs, to the removal of sugar-laden vending machines, teachers have always known that student behaviour and achievement is linked to food. With behaviour disorders there is a more urgent need to educate parents and children about the benefits of food that effect a slow release of energy throughout the day, rather than a short burst of sugar that results in a 'crash' shortly afterwards.

For students with behaviour disorders there is strong evidence that nutrition can treat not just the symptom but also the root cause.

Research evidence

Alexandra Richardson studied more than 100 children of normal ability in mainstream schools in County Durham, who were underachieving and suspected of being dyspraxic – that is, of having problems with coordination or motor skills. In some cases, the children were also disruptive.

Once they had been assessed, they were divided into two groups for a randomised double-blind, placebo-controlled trial. Half of them were given fish oils high in Omega-3 essential fats for three months. The other half were given placebos. Some 40% of the children given supplements made dramatic improvements in reading and spelling, averaging progress of more than nine months in just three months. The control group made just the normal progress of three months.

Although none had been diagnosed as suffering from ADHD, a third were found to have sufficient problems to put them in this category. But when given fish oils, half of them made so much progress they no longer counted as having attention disorders – a change on a par with improvements made when children are prescribed stimulant drugs such as Ritalin.

TV

Teachers experience the effects of television on children every day. These effects range from seemingly harmless play-acting Power Rangers in the playground, to changes in language brought about by American 'gangsta' slang, to irritable students suffering from sleep deprivation. There is mounting evidence that watching too much television is changing the way in which children concentrate and learn.

> '[Television] stunts the development of children's brains, increases the likelihood of children developing ADHD and may permanently hinder children's educational progress.'
>
> (Dr Aric Sigman, 2005, Remotely Controlled)

In particular, television has been shown to have a particularly detrimental effect on younger children, damaging and changing the nature and span of attention. Like fast food that has been developed to keep people eating, television has developed refined techniques to keep people watching. The most common problem seems to be the proliferation of screens in children's bedrooms. Survey your class and you may be surprised just how many students have got televisions (cable-ready with 50 channels), computers and game consoles that they can watch and play in bed. Often without parental control, they are able to access programming throughout the night, receiving images that are designed for an adult audience. There are obvious issues of access to unsuitable materials and associated concerns about students not giving time to reading, sleep, outdoor play, having conversations with parents and siblings, being comfortable with silence and developing their own inner voice and thoughts. In many homes the television is the first thing to be switched on in the morning and the last thing to be switched off at night. Even when families leave the house, access to television and new media is unrestricted: in cars, in school cafeterias, on mobile phones, on aeroplanes, handheld DVD and hard drives, etc. With the arrival of interactive whiteboards and computer projection, some classrooms are beginning to resemble mini lecture theatres. The teacher and student are forced to spend a great deal, if not all, of the lesson staring at a screen – both of whom for different reasons will have spent most of the previous evening staring at a screen. Is it really benefiting children to create and develop their understanding of the world through a series of computer and media screens? For parents to use television to rear their offspring? For teachers to rely solely on electronic media to present ideas?

Mobile phones

Mobile phones are now causing new behaviour challenges for teachers: receiving and making calls in lessons, sending and receiving texts, accessing the web, playing games, taking photographs, recording audio and video. Then there are the associated problems of theft, selling and receiving stolen phones and sim cards, 'happy slapping' videos (another great media catchphrase in the tradition of 'joyriding'), malicious text bullying and candid photography. At a time when schools are struggling to meet the behavioural needs of students, the advent of the mobile phone in schools has not helped. Some schools have banned mobile phones only to find students covertly using them, and parents undermining the rules by phoning them in the middle of the day. If we could step away from the fear and paranoia that drives parents to insist on direct and immediate contact with their child (in part perpetuated by the commercial interests of the mobile companies) perhaps the Government could allow schools to use signal blockers (widely available but currently illegal in the UK) so that the mobile becomes redundant for communicating with the outside world in the classroom. These devices are cheap, effective and would solve the challenges in the classroom at a stroke. Teachers could resume their role *in loco parentis*, students could put their social lives on hold while they are learning, we could use the features of the technology for recording learning (photo, video, audio recordings, etc.) and everyone would accept that there is an appropriate time and place for communicating with the outside world.

Why not try this?

The graph on the next page is to be filled out by the student (there are printable versions on www.pearsoned.co.uk/essentialguides). Look at the list overleaf and together decide which labels are most useful for the Y-axis, or create your own. You should choose two different areas for focus during one lesson. The student plots on the chart every five minutes during the lesson giving a rating of 1–10 for both areas of focus. You might decide to do it over one lesson or a series of lessons, then meet with the student to discuss the outcome. There will be targets for the students that arise, but this task should also allow you to reflect on your own teaching and management of the individual.

→

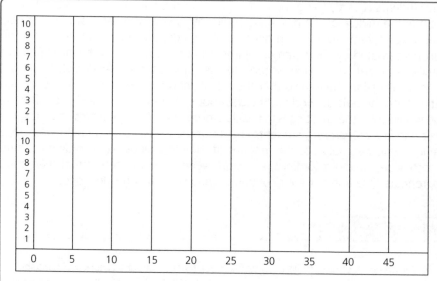

List of possible labels for the Y-axis:

- The task
- My work
- My behaviour
- My concentration
- My teacher
- Myself
- My control
- My language
- How angry I feel
- How calm I feel
- How happy I feel
- My motivation
- My enthusiasm
- My understanding of the work

Key ideas summary

Key idea	Benefit for the teacher	Benefit for the students
Being flexible in your design and application of rewards and sanctions.	Allows the teacher to change the frequency and level of intervention to best meet the needs of the individual.	Being part of discussions on rewards and sanctions. The student, whose behaviour is not linear, appreciates the flexibility the teacher is able to allow.
Aiming for success over a longer timescale.	The teacher is able to plan for smaller changes over a longer period of time and avoid the frustration of expecting immediate change.	Gives the students more time to unravel learned negative behaviours.
Using short-term targets.	Targets are set at the task level and the student is closely monitored. Short-term targets encourage sustained periods of appropriate behaviour.	Teacher attention has a higher frequency, targets are more immediate and there is less opportunity to drift off task.
Careful consideration of seating plan.	Students can be positioned so that they are able to support rather than disrupt the learning of their neighbour. Peer groups who spark off each other can be separated.	Students have the opportunity to learn away from their friends and integrate with other students.
Measured responses to inappropriate or extreme behaviour.	Keeps your emotional brain in check and avoids repeated confrontation with students.	They are able to predict your responses. Their extreme behaviour does not elicit the extreme response that they desire.
Proactively developing a relationship with the student.	Builds trust with the student. Allows greater understanding of individual needs and circumstances.	Builds trust with the teacher which can lead to respect. They begin to listen to and value your opinions. It matters when you are unhappy about their behaviour.
Seeking advice and reporting back to senior colleagues, outside agencies and parents.	The teacher doesn't feel isolated and learns from the other professionals.	The student sees the teacher as part of a team of people working in their best interests. The student is accountable for their behaviour in class to a wider audience.

Practical strategies for Primary, Secondary, FE and HE

Primary

Deal or no deal?

The offer of a deal is tempting. It suggests compromise to the child; it signals that the adults are prepared to listen and encourages the child's positive expectation of what is to come. The truth is that many people will accept the idea of a deal without even knowing the details. 'Do you want to make a deal?' almost always gets a good response and played correctly allows you to suggest the parameters. The lightening of your tone and apparent reasonableness may allow you to frame the deal so that you haven't actually moved from your original position. It also allows some breathing space from the tedious roundabout of 'I'm not', 'You are', 'I'm not', 'You are'.

> 'You have made it really clear that you would rather not get dressed for PE (climbing out of the window was a bit of a giveaway), yet I have a deal for you that is going to make you really smile. Do you want to make a deal?'

There is skill in brokering and sealing the deal without bribery or resorting to threats. 'You know that good things happen when you are caught following the rules' is different in intention to 'Get dressed and I will give you this bag of money'. Just as reminding children of their previous appropriate behaviour, 'You got dressed so quickly and happily yesterday', is very different from 'I wish you could behave like Kylie, look, isn't she a shining example of what you should be?'

By offering a deal you are finding a different route to the same destination. Manage the conversation with skill and finding different routes will become a natural first response to defiant behaviour. The urge to bulldoze the child into behaving will subside and you will begin to enjoy the art of managing behaviour.

Secondary

Improving extremely challenging behaviour

Identify and encourage a significant mentor:

- Refuse to accept the 'front' of youth/criminal/gang culture from the person

- Plan to interrupt learned patterns of behaviour
- Intensively and overtly model appropriate behaviour
- Actively build mutual trust
- Address the student's internal voice
- Contribute to and manage a multi-agency approach
- Find the hook or convince the student you have found one
- Direct support to address external issues affecting behaviour
- Stay calm
- Be more than reasonable
- Remain empathetic, consistent and fair
- Control/suppress natural instincts
- Deliver engaging lessons
- Deal with parents
- Hold on to your sanity

FE and HE

'I am sorry that you are having a bad day', shifts the responsibility for the behaviour to the student. Delivered kindly it can soften an entrenched position and make the consequences seem an inevitable result of the behaviour without attacking the student's identity.

30 days to make a change

Think about the changes that you would like to make in how you manage more extreme/challenging behaviour. This might relate to an individual student, class or context. Commit to the new strategies for 30 days to allow them to embed into practice and your own teaching style.

In 30 days I will walk into work and ....

....

....

....

....

Make a commitment to try some of the strategies that have been suggested in this chapter.

My personal resolutions are:

1 _____   Review date _____

2 _____   Review date _____

3 _____   Review date _____

Collaborating with other adults

Seeking support: why, when and how

'We are all here on earth to help others; what on earth the others are here for I don't know.'

(W. H. Auden)

The principle

As a teacher, the students in your class are your responsibility. You alone are responsible for managing their behaviour in your classroom. It is your right to seek support from senior colleagues and parents when necessary, but you need to manage this support carefully. If you delegate responsibility for managing the behaviour of students in your class to colleagues it will weaken your relationship with the class, as well as your status and authority. You have a responsibility to remain a part of the management of even the most challenging students, even if that student has been removed from the class and is being dealt with by someone else.

Reflecting on practice

It goes something like this: a student behaves appallingly in class and a senior manager/site security is called for. With your temper only just in check, you explain what has happened and the student is taken away to receive appropriate punishment. You return to your classroom, satisfied that the student has been disciplined, and try to calm down yourself and the rest of the class. The next time you see this student is at the start of your next lesson together. The student enters holding a report card and refuses to engage with you or the lesson. Another incident occurs and the colleague is summoned and again removes the student. You complain that nothing has changed and the support you have received is not solving anything. You even start to believe that the student in question is 'unteachable' and there is a general grunt of agreement beneath mugs of tea in the staffroom. The student clearly resents the way in which he has been treated and most of his resentment is directed at you.

The practice

Think carefully about the process you go through before calling for support in lessons. Senior colleagues will rightly be suspicious if you regularly call on them within the first two minutes or if they need to return to your classroom every five minutes throughout the lesson. It is easy to infer from this that you wish to pass responsibility for managing the behaviour of your students to a third party. If your call for support is because of persistent low-level disruption, make sure that you have calmly exhausted a range of strategies and at each stage given the student the space and time to make better choices. If you are calling for support because of a single incident of extreme behaviour, don't try to address it with the student when support arrives; wait until everyone has had longer to calm down and reflect on what has happened.

When support arrives speak to the colleague privately and discreetly, preferably away from the student. Try to be flexible in the support requested from the teacher. It may not be possible or indeed appropriate for the student to be removed for the whole lesson or even part of it. Often the arrival of another member of staff who can support high-level sanctions is enough to encourage the student to modify their behaviour. Keep your conversation with the 'on call' teacher/security calm, focused on observed behaviours and non-judgemental. Try asking for advice rather than demanding specific and immediate actions. Weigh up your next move carefully. Do you really want the student removed or is there a chance that they may be able to rectify their behaviour? What outcome are you trying to achieve? What, if anything, do you want the supporting colleague to reinforce?

If the student is removed from the lesson make time before the next lesson with the same class to speak to the student calmly and quietly. This meeting is vital. Make the time to do it and the investment will pay off. Don't be put off by the number of other incidents the student may have been involved in that day or find excuses not to do it. Your primary concern should be the student's behaviour in *your* class. Try dropping in on their tutor period, arranging to have five minutes with the student out of a colleague's lesson or meeting them at the entrance to the site the next morning.

By meeting the student, calmly explaining why he had to be removed and what behaviour you expect to see next time, you are sending a clear message to the student: you want him to be a part of the class, you care about his learning and you are responsible for the behaviour of all students in your class. This message may not filter through in the first instance but over time it will become clear. You will feel involved in his reintegration and your relationship with him will develop. You will be able to refer to the conversation you have had in future incidents and the class will begin to understand that you use support from other colleagues as a temporary measure and not as a permanent attempt at a solution.

TOP TIP!

Keeping accurate, dated and detailed records on student behaviour means that you have valuable evidence that can be used in a variety of ways:

- *To support your requests for additional internal support*
- *To look for patterns of behaviour – days of the week, times in the day*
- *To discuss with parents*
- *To share with the student*
- *To support requests for support from external agencies.*

It can, however, be very time-consuming to make accurate records on each student and you may find it better simply to begin making detailed records on individuals as soon as you notice sequences of poor behaviour.

Watch out for ...

- Deferring responsibility to senior managers too quickly, too often or too publicly: 'When your Head of Year hears about this ...', or, 'I'm going straight to the Principal's office.'

- The student who has been excluded after an incident in your lesson. His feelings of resentment are likely to be stronger and he will have had a greater input from senior colleagues and parents. Ask to be a part of the reintegration process and the negotiations with the student even if the exclusion is bundled with other incidents.

Reflecting on practice

Schools and colleges should have set procedures for calling a colleague, usually a senior member of staff or site security, to an incident in a lesson. What is not often discussed is the management of the arrival of the 'on-call' adult.

The following list of responses was generated by 120 teachers on a training day after enacting and reflecting on classic 'on call' scenarios.

What the class teacher can do before the 'on-call' teacher arrives

- Remove the student from the situation, if appropriate.
- Quietly ask the student to pack things ready to leave.
- Back off, don't continue the confrontation.
- Keep in mind that the student's behaviour is not a personal attack on you (unless it clearly is) and that the sanction is the result of their poor choices.
- Remember, students need to be removed to give them the time and space to calm down, not as a punishment in itself.

Class teacher's responsibilities

- Don't discuss the behaviour publicly, either in front of the class or in front of the 'on-call' teacher.
- Demonstrate appropriate behaviour by remaining calm.
- Have the conversation with the 'on-call' teacher in private.
- Think about your responsibility for the situation: how can you address the problem in future lessons?
- Speak personally to the student about the incident at a later date.

- Agree a positive target for future behaviour.
- Only ask things of the 'on-call' teacher that they will be able to deliver.
- Keep the explanation of the incident brief and to the point.
- Record strategies that you have used with the student before calling for support.
- Do not use the arrival of the 'on-call' teacher to publicly vent your anger at all the ills of the class 'and Boyce has been just as bad, yes, you and your mate Jez, neither of you have done anything since September … etc., etc.'

Responsibilities of the 'on-call' teacher

- Approach the situation calmly.
- Model good behaviour for the rest of the students.
- Reinforce good behaviour in others through praise.
- Don't undermine the teacher.
- Listen carefully to what the teacher tells you about the incident.
- Don't judge the situation there and then; ask for accurate records.

Why not try this?

Photocopy the list below and either attach it to your incident report pro-forma or use it as a stand-alone. When an incident occurs that requires the support of a senior colleague, hand the checklist to them so that they can see the strategies that you have used with the student. This checklist is useful as an aide-mémoire for yourself and a prompt sheet when discussing the incident with the student after the lesson. It also serves to remind senior colleagues that you are using positive behaviour-management techniques and places the responsibility for the incident firmly with the student.

Behaviour management strategies used	Tick
Acknowledged good behaviour choices	
Spoke to the student privately and at eye level	
Was consistent in application of classroom behaviour plan	
Gave the student time and space to rectify behaviour	
Listened to the student	

Behaviour management strategies used	Tick
Referred to the learning rituals (posted on the wall)	
Gave a verbal warning	
_____ sanction given	
_____ sanction given	
Student was moved away from friends	
Used positive reinforcement to get the student back on task	
Drew back from confrontation	
Student given 'time out' to calm down	

Key ideas summary

Key idea	Benefit for the teacher	Benefit for the students
Teachers have responsibility for the students in their care; this responsibility cannot be delegated or passed over.	The teacher's leadership of behaviour management is not undermined by the delegation of responsibility.	Students know that they are accountable to the class teacher for their behaviour in class.
When incidents occur make time to see the student and renegotiate expectations.	The teacher is able to reinforce the rules of the classroom and build their understanding of the student's needs.	Students are certain that poor choices in behaviour will be followed up. They have an opportunity to have their say.
Ensure that before you call for support you have calmly and fairly applied your framework for behaviour for behaviour management and exhausted positive strategies.	When colleagues understand that you are using positive strategies and structured interventions they are able to feel confident in offering the support requested.	Students are treated according to the agreed framework management; when support is called it is clear to everyone that it is necessary.

Strategies for Primary, Secondary, FE and HE

Primary

Take care not just to seek support for managing inappropriate behaviour. Forewarn and negotiate with senior colleagues so that you can send students to them for praise or ask them to drop in to your lesson to deliver rewards.

Secondary

Keeping a clear focus on your own teaching does not preclude working as part of a staff team to improve behaviour. In all institutions, and particularly in those with significant behaviour issues, there will be a small number of key staff who have a major influence on students. Align yourself with one of these key members of staff. This might be a formal arrangement where you seek regular support and advice, or more likely an informal one, where you ask them to pass by or visit your classroom at critical times. Students will recognise the alliances that staff form and may adjust their decisions on behaviour accordingly. That is why the supply teacher who has no regular team within the school is often identified by students as an easy target. The NQT who is mentored by a senior teacher is a more risky proposition for students choosing to cause disruption.

FE and HE

When you notice a pattern of inappropriate behaviour emerging, start making a chronological record. You might choose to share this with the student, use it as a basis for discussion around appropriate boundaries and as evidence to seek appropriate support. From recording those students who persistently arrive late, to noting students who are disengaging and keeping a keen eye on persistent low-level disruption, having clear, non-judgmental evidence is vital if you are to talk about the specific behaviours that need addressing.

30 days to make a change

Think about the changes that you would like to make in how you manage support. This might relate to an individual student, class or context. Commit to the new strategies for 30 days to allow them to embed into practice and your own teaching style.

In 30 days I will walk into work and ....

....

....

....

....

Make a commitment to try some of the strategies that have been suggested in this chapter.

My personal resolutions are:

1 _____   Review date _____

2 _____   Review date _____

3 _____   Review date _____

Teaching partnerships: collaborative approaches with the LSA and other adults

'If we are together nothing is impossible. If we are divided all will fail.'

(Winston Churchill)

The principle

The adults working alongside the teacher (be they parents, learning mentors, teaching assistants, other teachers or visitors) have a responsibility to use the existing structure for behaviour management in your classroom. If the adults within the room are speaking with one voice and are committed to the same goals, the management of behaviour is streamlined. If one is poorly briefed, or uses behaviour-management techniques that are not in line with the other's, then the classroom becomes divided. Some students will take advantage of the divide and dance in the gaps of inconsistent practice.

The practice

Before another adult comes into your classroom to work with students, you must meet with them. I know that is easy to say, and I know just how many meetings are worthless, yet this meeting has real value – not just in informing them of the content of the lesson but for some simple agreements to be made on the management of behaviour. Assuming that the adult will be in your classes fairly regularly, they need a voice in the classroom that they can develop to an equal status. It is not in anyone's best interests to leave other adults trying to employ their own strategies in isolation or to emphasise any difference in status.

If the teacher is the only one that applies the behaviour plan then other adults will be viewed as having a lower status. If you can raise the status of the assistant in the students' eyes, you will benefit from the presence of another confident adult in your class. As a practical step you might have a formal agreement that both of you can deliver the first two rewards and sanctions on the hierarchy or that you will consult each other when a student is given a 'time out'. This will form a good foundation on which to build equality.

Your management of adults in the classroom is worth the investment of time. I realise that is seems easier to nod a hello and leave support assistants sitting at the back trying to stop Patrick and his friends chewing the curtains, but you are wasting one of your most valuable resources. Organise a regular time when you can sit down and talk once a week or fortnight. Plan to discuss key behaviour strategies in each meeting as well as the immediate business of lesson content, groupings and responsibilities. This needs to be a two-way conversation, and alongside following your own agenda, you will want to listen to feedback on how your teaching is received. The perspective of the teaching assistant is unique; they often receive the lesson with the students and see the students' private reactions to it. Being open to their comments will enable you to better tailor your teaching style to meet the needs of individual classes.

Although many teaching assistants have a large repertoire of behaviour-management skills and will have some training in behaviour management, many will have little experience in managing students in a classroom environment. Your guidance and training, starting from simple agreements, can make a huge difference to how other adults perceive their role and feel empowered to take responsibility for managing behaviour. As the leader in the classroom you need to invest time in training other adults to employ strategies and techniques that work with your classes.

The balance of power should change when there is more than one significant adult in the room. Suddenly there are fewer hiding places for those trying to avoid engaging in the lesson. There are fewer dark corners as the adults work the room, managing behaviour and learning as a team. The student–staff ratio is halved and, when used successfully, additional staffing can reduce the number of students who need your attention and the number who disrupt.

There may be some adults working in your classroom who have a remit to work with one individual. Although some students welcome this one-to-one interaction, it can become frustrating for them if they are always sitting and working with the same adult. Their separation from the rest of the class can be intensified, and it is easy for them to feel that they are being continuously watched and guarded. It is important that adults who are supporting individual students also have time away and opportunities to work with others in the class. This is not to undermine their role with the individual, because this will remain their primary focus, but to give both parties time apart and allow the student to engage in independent thought, learning and socialisation. If an adult is attached to a student for every lesson, neither has the space to develop their own learning and practice.

TOP TIP!

If you feel that you need to maintain control over higher-level sanctions (either temporarily or permanently) you will need to agree a level at which a student's behaviour is referred to you. Create a subtle mechanism for the other adult to inform you when students reach, say, Level 4 on your sanctions hierarchy; pass a note, whisper the student's name, write a note on the desk, etc. Discussing such instances in front of the class risks confrontation or unwelcome intervention from other students.

Watch out for ...

- Adults becoming involved in public arguments with students.
- Adults threatening students with a higher authority than your own: 'I'll tell the Deputy Head about this.'
- Being drawn into public three-way confrontations between student, teacher and assistant.
- Making sure other adults demonstrate appropriate behaviour for the students. This includes: turning up on time, with appropriate equipment, mobile phone switched off, not leaving the classroom during the lesson, listening when one person is speaking to the class.

Reflecting on practice

When other adults take over – a lesson observed

The start of the lesson was fairly calm, a struggle to keep students calm but nothing out of the ordinary. I had already noted how quiet the teacher's voice was and was interested in how the class was responding to her. There was off-task behaviour but it was not noisy and the pockets of disturbance were kept fairly isolated. As I wondered if her vocal softness was a deliberate ploy or not, the door flew open. Things were about to get a whole lot louder.

Addressing the boys at the back from the door, the teaching assistant cut across the whole class and began her behaviour-management strategy. This, it turned out, was to confront each and every misdemeanour with the tone and physical language that you would avoid witnessing on the streets. The teacher had no chance. All attention was on the assistant, who would launch into aggressive personal attacks on the boys at the most inopportune moments. The tension in the room was palpable as some of the larger boys became genuinely affronted at the attacks, which were given an anti-male bias, 'You going to be a stupid boy forever, yes boy, you ain't no man (etc.)'. The rest of the class tried to shield themselves from the shrapnel and the teacher was left ignored and unheard. I was dumbfounded and was finding it difficult to remain the silent observer. It soon became clear, however, that this lesson was no different to the ones that had gone before. The teaching assistant knew that intimidation worked for her outside the school gates and saw no reason why it should not work within them. She was indeed a frightening presence in the room.

In discussion with the teacher, I discovered that the two had never met to discuss roles in the lesson, and that the present situation had been going on for a number of weeks. The teacher felt that she needed more help with managing student behaviour; I suggested some management of the teaching assistant would be a better starting point. To her credit she was aware of what was happening but the teaching assistant frightened her as well and she was worried about having to approach her on her own.

Most of the adults that work in schools have little formal training in managing behaviour and are forced to guess what is expected of them in classrooms. It is hardly surprising that they act inappropriately when thrown in at the deep end. Although there is some responsibility on the employer to provide appropriate training, in practice it is the teacher who becomes trainer as they know the potential benefit to teaching, learning and behaviour.

Why not try this?

Use this checklist to generate discussion, introduce basic strategies and create a simple agreement between all of the adults working in your classroom.

A joint approach to managing behaviour:

- These rewards and sanctions should be applied by all adults ...
- These rewards and sanctions are the responsibility of the lead teacher ...
- What happens if one of us makes a mistake when applying the plan?
- Which specific students will each of us monitor?
- The agreed procedure for sharing information on behaviour issues in the classroom is ...
- The following students respond particularly well to positive reinforcement, praise and reward ...
- What roles should each of us take in a critical incident?

Key ideas summary

Key idea	Benefit for the teacher	Benefit for the students
Meet and plan with all adults before they enter your classroom to work with students.	The teacher can make informed decisions on how to utilise the skills of support staff. The adults can decide how to manage behaviour together.	The students know there is a consistent approach in the classroom from all adults.
Invest time in training adults who regularly work with your classes.	The teacher can share knowledge of strategies that work and how to employ them effectively. The supporting teacher develops their skills in managing behaviour as part of a team and independently.	Students are managed by increasingly skilled, calm and subtle interventions by the support teacher.
All adults work within the agreed framework for behaviour management.	The adults maintain consistency in behaviour management; the rules apply regardless of whom students are working with.	Students are not able to exploit perceived or real differences in rules and expectations between adults.

→

Key idea	Benefit for the teacher	Benefit for the students
All adults have responsibility for delivering rewards and sanctions.	The support teacher is empowered and encouraged to use positive behaviour-management strategies.	Students know that there are positive outcomes for following the directions of the support teacher.
An adult assigned to work with an individual is not precluded from helping others.	The teacher is able to use some professional judgement in the distribution of additional support.	Students are able to approach the support teacher for help; the focus student is given some space to breathe, think and make mistakes.

Strategies for Primary, Secondary, FE and HE

Primary

Arm your teaching assistant with a pad of positive notes, wad of stickers and a special stamp and share the responsibility for catching students behaving appropriately. Make sure that between you all of the children have been seen within one lesson by checking that each has two stamps.

Secondary, FE and HE

If you find it impossible to meet with learning support assistants before the lesson try to routinely take five minutes to discuss the lesson that is to be delivered while the students complete their starter activity. I know that it would be better to have this conversation before the lesson, I also know how difficult this is to do on a daily basis.

30 days to make a change

Think about the changes that you would like to make in how you manage support in the classroom. This might relate to an individual student, class or context. Commit to the new strategies for 30 days to allow them to embed into practice and your own teaching style.

In 30 days I will walk into work and ....

....

....

....

....

Make a commitment to try some of the strategies that have been suggested in this chapter.

My personal resolutions are:

1 _____   Review date _____

2 _____   Review date _____

3 _____   Review date _____

Nurturing the support of parents, mentors and the wider community

'I didn't have any concept of age or authority. I remember realising, Oh, the world has rules and we don't.'

(Moon Unit Zappa – Daughter of Frank Zappa)

The principle

Parents are like their children. Some are enthusiastic, committed and passionate about education. Some would rather not engage with it at all. They prefer to hide and throw insults over the barricades. Rather like their children! Engaging willing parents is not the challenge. Engaging and communicating with those who have good reason to disengage with education and authority is so much harder and much less attractive.

Parents have a responsibility to support the education of their children, and work in partnership with the school or college. There is a great deal that we can learn from the parents, and vice versa. Teachers need to nurture and encourage communication with parents who renege on these responsibilities. If contact with parents is always about negative aspects of the student's behaviour, support will ebb away. The more parents can understand the behaviour-management frameworks and strategies used in the classroom, the easier it is to communicate accurately with them.

The practice

The old metaphor of the student as a three-legged stool supported by school/college, home and community is still relevant today. Take a leg away and the student starts to wobble. Work out how to communicate effectively with and engage reluctant parents and you can give stability back to the wobbliest students. Parents are responsible for managing the behaviour of their children, but this is shared with the school or college and the people who interact with the child in the community.

Parents who don't engage in their child's education do so for a reason. They have made a conscious decision to separate school/college and home. There are many reasons why this happens: the parents may have had a negative experience of education, they may not know how to become more involved, they may lack understanding about the role of the parent, are exasperated at their child's behaviour, are angry for some past miscommunication, etc. Regardless of the perceived commitment of the parent, you have a responsibility to communicate your expectations clearly. Proactively engaging support from parents/carers is in your own best interests and in the best interests of the student. The additional benefit is that many parents looking for help and advice on how to manage behaviour in the home may adapt ideas that are being used in the classroom.

Drawing in reluctant parents might take more than just designing events and inviting them in. It will certainly need more than an annual sales pitch or open day. It is vital that communication with parents/carers is regular, positive and gentle. Create triggers that demand a drip feed of personal contact with parents. Design a strategy that ensures positive contact at least three times a term. Two positive referrals would trigger a phone call home, a good day on report demands a text message, teachers aim to give at least five positive notes home per week, emailed newsletters automatically sent every half term. A series of disruptive lessons always demands contact with home but when contact with parents is always about negative aspects of the child's behaviour or learning, support will ebb away.

If you are going to change classroom practice and school policy regarding behaviour then the parents must be communicated with, consulted and engaged. The more parents can understand what happens in the classroom the more they are likely to engage with their children, the homework, teachers, etc. I often led parents' meetings where we have encouraged the parents to come and experience the training that the teachers have had. The whole evening seems to be focused on the children, the teachers and the classroom. The environment is 'safe' for parents who look for reasons to stay away. The focus is on what happens in the classroom, but it is also a route to send some of the good practice into the home. As I talk about new policy and practice I see parents looking at each other and saying 'we could do that at home', and 'maybe we were wrong to ban TV forever!' At that point I know that the message has been sent safely. I know that it is more likely to be acted upon. Parents who looked anxious at the start of the evening go away with a few more strategies to try.

I have listened to colleagues despairing at the lack of contact from parents; bemoaning the lack of support and showing frustration at the absence of any consistent approach between home and school or college. Yet when asked what they have done to build a relationship, the responsibility has always rested with the parent: 'I write but they don't reply, I invite but they refuse, I call but they don't answer.' I have always taken a more pragmatic approach. If my attempts to communicate and engage the parents don't bear fruit, then I will be proactive. I will take the initiative and, yes, knock on the door and introduce myself.

If you want to engage with people who would rather eat glass than even step inside a classroom, you might have to meet them on their own terms. You might have to get together with them in a safer place and communicate without the protection of the institution; yes, you may even need to visit them at home.

Teachers who go the extra mile to persist with disengaged parents know the benefits. They know that the one of the most effective behaviour-management tools they can draw upon is the relationship with the parent. As teachers nurture this bond with the home, wobbly students stop rocking and the classroom behaviour starts to stabilise.

You may choose to write to all parents of the students you teach informing them of the rules, rewards and sanctions that operate in your classroom and explaining a few of the behaviour-management strategies that you are using. Thereafter your communication can take many forms: positive notes home, parents' evenings, positive phone calls home, report cards to be countersigned, impositions (extra work to be completed at home and delivered the following morning) to be checked, phone calls asking for support, etc. Try to make sure there is some balance between your communications. When you ask for additional support and input because of a period of inappropriate behaviour, make sure that they are also informed when the student's behaviour improves. For students who are persistently disruptive you will need to sow the seeds of a longer relationship with the parent(s), remembering that you are unlikely to be the only teacher/professional that the parents need to find time for. Try asking for advice and support rather than telling parents what you want them to do. Even if they have no immediate solutions it will open up a dialogue and make it clear that you wish to work in partnership with them.

TOP TIP!

You will find that starting communication with parents with positive news about the behaviour of their child is a much easier way in. It also makes them more disposed to support you when there are problems. If you contact parents too late they may question why they were not informed earlier and be shocked at the list of crimes they now need to deal with.

Make sure that you are aware of any safeguarding issues before you rush to contact home to report bad news about a student. In a small minority of homes a negative communication from school can result in an overreaction that leads to physical aggression. If you know this to be the case, seek advice from a senior colleague. If you are meeting with parents for the first time consider doing so with a colleague present.

If you are going to communicate effectively with home you will need up-to-date contact information from parents. At the same time it is useful to ask how they would prefer to be contacted. When you are communicating bad news, consider that letters can be intercepted, phone messages ignored, etc. Try to find the most secure and immediate method of communication that removes responsibility from the student and guarantees that you can not only get a message to the child's home, but also receive one back. You may choose to use a separate school email address or call a mobile number at an agreed time. Think carefully about the timing of your communication: it may well affect the way in which the information is received and acted upon. You may choose to make contact initially simply to organise a better time to speak at length. This guarantees that the parent will be prepared for the conversation and have time for it.

When there is a bond between home and school the child will see that his behaviour and its consequences are not confined to the classroom. The relationships I built up with parents were one of the most effective behaviour-management tools I could draw upon. I would often phone home before the student arrived there or on some memorable occasions be sitting drinking tea with the parent when the child arrived home from school. Once students know that a positive relationship exists and that consistent and regular contact is maintained he will check his behaviour carefully and modify responses accordingly.

Most students prefer to separate their home life from their life in school. They are often keen to avoid direct discussion between parents and teachers; I remember as a student the anxiety the build-up to parents' evenings elicited. Knowing that all of my sins would be laid bare and I would have to confront them in front of my teachers and parents was not a comfortable experience. Try to establish individual rapport with parents so they know who they are dealing with; they can put a face to a name and over time build up trust in their child's teacher.

TOP TIP!

Find regular opportunities to communicate with parents about the child's progress. Don't wait for the parent to come to you at parents' evenings but go over and introduce yourself. Give regular feedback if a child is on subject report, send a note home, or pick up the phone, 'Just giving you a quick call to let you know how Joshua is getting on ...'

When you meet parents to discuss their child don't launch straight into the discussion that you really want to have. Often both parent and teacher come to the meeting with some apprehension and frustration that needs to be diffused to allow each to relax and share concerns calmly. It is your responsibility to make sure that the meeting goes well and that there is a positive outcome. Avoid discussion about the weather and obvious 'small talk'. Instead, try asking after the family, talk about their recent house move or older siblings' progress at university; show genuine interest and concern about their lives and reinforce your role as a caring professional who is working in the best interests of their child. This will put the parent(s) at ease and you may learn something new that informs your work with the student. Try to connect your concerns about the child's behaviour with your care for their learning and ask for advice on 'what works well at home'. Focus on a partnership approach and look for ways of quickly and efficiently connecting rewards and sanctions at school with those at home.

Watch out for ...

- Becoming too familiar and informal with parents – certainly in the early stages of the relationship they may interpret your throwaway remarks as an indicator of your level of professionalism and commitment to their child. Keep your conversation friendly but always professional and don't take risks by being indiscreet or flippant.

- Making assumptions about the domestic circumstances of a student. Your complaints about the lack of homework may seem trivial when you discover just how many people are living in one house or that there has been a recent bereavement in the family.

- 'Telling' parents how to manage the behaviour of their child. Ask for their advice, share some things that seem to be working in the classroom and search for a dialogue that involves everyone in finding strategies that work.

Reflecting on practice

Meet the parent

As a new teacher I was wary of parents. My own lack of understanding about parenting and limited teaching experience made me apprehensive. Tales of parents assaulting staff and trashing the Headteacher's office made me think they were best left alone. After all, I wasn't a social worker and I didn't need to know them to teach their children.

Damien's roaring – yes, roaring – was becoming a real problem. It was loud and persistent and timed for maximum impact in the quiet of the classroom jungle. He had reached the end of every sanction list, class report, school report, broken every classroom rule and now had decided that roaring was the way to go. Talking to the Head of Year, I asked about what sort of home life Damien had and what influence it might be having on his behaviour. I knew that the Head of Year had close contact with parents: they were difficult but she was an extremely skilled operator. 'Come and see,' was her reply. I was not convinced it was a good idea, but I figured that I would be fairly safe with her leading. This would be my first home visit: colleagues gently advised me that it was a road to nowhere.

Damien's house was on a large estate; rundown, sprawling, shops behind steel shutters, burnt out cars, etc. Not somewhere that anyone would choose to live. I had driven around the estate after I had accepted the post, making a mental note to do things the other way around next time, and this was the first time I had seen the houses at close quarters. Walking into the living room I was struck by the smell of dogs (there were five large ones), the noise of the younger children (there were four of them) and the sight of the sofa overflowing with clothes, food, rubbish, etc. In an instant I had a better understanding of Damien. In one moment I realised that his behaviour had more meaning, and even if I couldn't work out the psychology of it, I knew that there was a connection with his home life. His mother apologised profusely, but she was on her own and she could no longer control his behaviour. I explained the problems, she offered sympathy. Damien arrived back from collecting his sister, aged six, from school and the four of us tried to agree a way forward for the next week. He was not a malicious child; in fact he could be quite funny and the atmosphere was quite relaxed. I observed him playing with his younger brothers and sister and taking a great deal of pleasure from it. I saw a gentleness and kindness that was absent from his public persona.

I came away from the meeting much better educated about Damien, his home, the parallel homes of other students, the community and the desperation of some parents. I no longer trotted out the line about not being a

→

social worker, learned to be much slower in my judgement of students and began to look further than just the behaviour. My relationship with Damien was deepened; after all, out of all the teachers in the school, there was only the Head of Year and myself who had seen the other side of his world. Our eye contact had more meaning and although the journey was going to be a long one I knew that it would be easier than before. When colleagues complained that 'He might be alright in your lesson but he's now squawking and perching on the chair like a bird in mine,' I wanted to tell them why, but they would just call it 'social work'. For me the extra investment of time was paying dividends, my classes could get back to learning and Damien was slowly engaging in the lessons.

I later used the home visit to great effect, shooting round to Number 37 straight after school; I would be eating samosas, discussing Cat Stevens and Asif's behaviour as Asif walked in the door from school. I always took much enjoyment out of watching his face drop as he realised that school and home were no longer separate.

Why not try this?

Use the pro forma below to draft a letter to all parents informing them about the rules, rewards and sanctions that operate in your classroom. The letter will seek support and advice, open up a dialogue with home and prepare parents/guardians for your future communications.

Dear Parent/Guardian,

I would like to keep you up to date with some of the behaviour-management strategies that I am using with all students. If you have any advice on the strategies that work well for your child I would appreciate the feedback.

There are ..... (insert number) rules that operate in the classroom:

(Insert rules here)

When students follow the rules they are rewarded using the following steps:

(Insert rewards here)

If students choose not to follow the rules they can expect the following stepped sanctions:

(Insert sanctions here)

I have adopted this framework to make the classroom a positive, consistent and safe place in which to learn. Students have been reminded that the following behaviours fall outside of the stepped sanctions and will result in ..... (insert high-level sanction).

(Insert extreme behaviour here e.g. violent, racist or aggressive behaviour, swearing at the teacher, etc.)

I aim to tell you as soon as possible when students reach high-level sanctions or repeatedly make poor choices. I will also make sure that I inform you when your child is behaving well. You can expect me to:

(Send positive notes home, call you/text/email when students are doing well – do keep me updated with changes in contact information – let you know if your child starts making poor choices, be consistent and fair in my application of the rules, ask for advice when I need it)

If you could discuss this plan with your child at home it would really help them start to see the link between home and school.

Yours truly,

Key ideas summary

Key idea	Benefit for the teacher	Benefit for the students
Proactively nurturing and engaging support from parents.	By working in partnership you are making a clear connection between home and school for the student. You are able to call on support and advice when necessary.	Students are supported with increasing consistency, they are surrounded by agreed expectations.
Communicate with home regularly, with positive news and for seeking support; let students know that you are communicating directly.	If the teacher is communicating regularly with positive feedback it is easier to elicit support when needed.	Students know there is a direct link between the classroom and home; they use this knowledge when deciding whether to disrupt.
Ask for advice and support from parents rather than simply telling them what you want them to do.	The teacher can learn from the experiences at home. Parents will be more willing to listen if they have been listened to first.	As ideas are shared the partnership between home and school is developed; joint strategies for managing certain behaviours are agreed.
Check with an appropriate colleague before contacting home with bad news.	The teacher avoids prompting an unwanted reaction from home and is prepared for any hostility.	Vulnerable students are protected because information is communicated carefully and sensitively.
Ask parents how and when they prefer to be contacted.	The conversation is not rushed and there is more time to choose your words with care.	Students are not involved in running messages between home and school that can easily go astray.

Strategies for Primary, Secondary, FE and HE

Primary

Collect the email addresses of your parents by offering them a series of tips that parents can sign up to that are written by teachers, such as '20 ways to help your child at school'. Use an automatic mailer such as www.aweber.com and use the software to send parents an automatic email every week. Include examples of work and updates on the progress of the class. Encourage communication between parents and in turn promote further involvement in PTAs and parents' groups.

Secondary

A 'good news' phone call from a teacher on a Friday evening has a huge impact on a family and their weekend. Students will seek you out on a Monday morning to thank you. Set yourself a target of perhaps 3–5 phone calls that you will make to reinforce appropriate behaviour every week. In all our surveys of students the phone call home comes out as their favourite reward. Parents appreciate it too. It builds relationships and used well it can break down fears and preconceptions.

FE and HE

Find out for each student who the important or key people are. For some it will still be parents, for others their tutor or mentor. Knowing who to contact when there is a problem is as important as knowing where to send your good news. Older students might be old enough to live apart from their family but this does not mean that they are too old for others to hear of their achievements and celebrate with them.

30 days to make a change

Think about the changes that you would like to make in how you involve and engage reluctant parents. This might relate to an individual student, class or context. Commit to the new strategies for 30 days to allow them to embed into practice and your own teaching style.

In 30 days I will walk into work and ....

....

....

....

....

Make a commitment to try some of the strategies that have been suggested in this chapter.

My personal resolutions are:

1 _____   Review date _____

2 _____   Review date _____

3 _____   Review date _____

Specific situations

Supply teachers, cover supervisors and cover lessons

'On the whole human beings want to be good, but not too good and not quite all the time.'

(George Orwell)

The principle

Either as a supply teacher or covering lessons for a colleague, you are accountable for the management of the students within your care. You also have a responsibility to the regular teacher to ensure you maintain their expectations and quality of teaching. If you try to use cover lessons as an opportunity to catch up on your own work, there will inevitably be difficulties with challenging classes. Your teaching should be of the standard that you would expect from a teacher covering lessons in your absence. Sitting at the desk and marking books is simply not enough to ensure the students get their needs met. Maintaining control in another teacher's classroom environment with a different seating plan, unfamiliar students and in a subject you may have little confidence with, presents its own challenges. Behaviour management can be more complicated.

The practice

In order to manage the behaviour of students who are not familiar with your expectations, rules, rewards and sanctions, you need to work hard throughout the lesson but especially at the start. There will inevitably be some students who see an opportunity to avoid work. The questioning and negotiating with the cover teacher begins: 'Do we have to do any work today?', 'Have you got our books, because we don't have them?', 'Can we just talk for a bit?', 'Miss normally lets us keep our coats on', 'Have you got a girlfriend, sir?', etc. They can sense your frustration at being left with a subject you may have little knowledge of or confidence with. They know you are busy and will have work of your own that you would like to do. Many classes will have had a string of supply and cover teachers over an extended period of time. Some will have fought off all but the best supply staff and a few will rub their hands, smile knowingly and move directly to 'operation sabotage'.

You need to start at the door of the room, enthusiastically welcoming the students and addressing expectations before they enter. Give them clear instructions on the basic routines and show them that you are keen to lead the lesson for them. If you have never met the students before, giving them large sticky labels to write their names on is a good idea. It won't necessarily stop all students swapping names, but it will allow you to speak to the majority of students using their first names and more accurately record any incidents.

Your physical and verbal language is very important when meeting the cover class for the first time. They are watching to see just how committed to the lesson you are and how confident you feel. You performance is critical. Convince them early on that you are secure in the content, enthusiastic about the teaching and have an aura of calm surety. The anger and frustration that you may be feeling because you have been put on cover for the third time in two days should be hidden and left for another time. Just as hostility won't help to manage the behaviour of the class, neither will a passive attitude. The struggling supply teacher's passive cry of, 'Well, at least I am going to get paid at the end of the day', or 'If you don't want to learn I can't teach you', won't help your management of behaviour. Your energy levels need to be high. In fact, the energy you expend at the beginning of the lesson is an investment that is likely to pay off when the class are fully engaged in the task. Try surprising them with your enthusiasm for the lesson. It can be very infectious.

In the opening minutes of the lesson you need to make your expectations absolutely clear and model your response to appropriate and inappropriate behaviours. If there are no school-wide rules and sanctions, have a scaled-down version of the structures that operate in your own classroom with you. Keep this to a maximum of three rules and sanctions. Rather than listing the rewards, you can reveal these as the lesson develops.

Explain very briefly that you will be using this framework and then immediately reward two or three students who have followed your instructions from the beginning. I always find it useful to have tangible and high-level rewards, such as a positive notes or referral to a colleague whom the students know well. This may not match the rewards structure in your own classroom, but it will send a clear message to the students that making good choices in the cover lesson is worthwhile.

Strategy spotlight

An example of rules and consequences for a cover lesson or supply teacher:

Rules

1 Follow instructions fast

2 Stay on task

3 Work without disturbing others

Consequences

1 Verbal warning

2 One minute after class

3 Time out

The sanctions that you employ will need to be adjusted to make it clear to students that they can expect no leniency from you. It will also serve to refocus their attention and behaviour away from automatic responses to cover lessons.

TOP TIP!

Try using a countdown to get the attention of the class and immediately and sincerely reward those students who respond quickly, 'Thank you for showing me such respect, you haven't met me before and you are listening really well, I am really going to enjoy working with you today.' Directed, descriptive reinforcement may not feel natural but it works. It identifies the behaviours that you want to see, is open, honest, and makes you appear entirely fair, reasonable and trustworthy.

It is at this point in the lesson that you are likely to be able to predict problems with the seating arrangement. Explain to the class that you expect everyone to be working throughout and for this reason you may need to direct the seating. It is much easier to move students in the early stages of the lesson: it causes less disruption to the learning. If students complain that you are changing their usual seating plan, listen to what they are saying and be flexible enough to make a deal.

Is the work appropriate?

Cover supervisors know lessons can be sabotaged by the quality of the cover work and sometimes by the negative messages from the regular teacher: 'We did this last week', 'Please, no more word searches!', 'My group is away today and I can't work without them.' Covering lessons is hard enough but when the work has been set with little thought it can be like walking through treacle in ski boots. If you cover a lesson and the work is inappropriate, you need to speak to the regular teacher as soon as possible. Explain that you found the work difficult to follow and ask for more guidance and information the next time. There is not always time to negotiate with the regular teacher before covering their lesson, but you need to be consistent in your feedback to them. You should write them a note at the end of the lesson recording those students who received rewards and sanctions (purely for information rather than action). By demonstrating your commitment to their lesson you are building your relationship with the absent teacher and making them think twice before setting similar work in the future. If these discussions have no impact on the quality of cover work, you will need to consider approaching the teacher's line manager or a senior member of staff. This is particularly important when you are on long-term supply or regularly cover for an absent teacher.

Be prepared in case the cover work provided is of particularly poor quality, or there is none set. Having a back-up plan in your bag may save you and the lesson. If you decide early in the lesson to move away from the work set, your feedback to the regular teacher needs to gently explain why you felt it was necessary. If you are on long-term supply or covering for a long-term absence, the cover work is likely to be set by the head of department. In such cases it is important that you contribute to the planning of lessons, as the colleague setting the work will already have a heavy workload. Discharging the responsibility for cover work completely will do nothing to solve your management issues with the class.

Under no circumstances, no matter how frustrated you are, should you undermine the regular teacher in front of students. This might be as simple as displaying your displeasure at the quality of the cover work or rifling through the teacher's desk and complaining that there are no board pens in the drawers. The students have had more time to develop a relationship with their regular teacher and are likely to respond defensively to any negative comments. You have a professional duty to air your frustrations in an appropriate way and at an appropriate time.

TOP TIP!

At the end of the lesson, make a point of leaving the room tidy and organised. Finding your classroom in a disorganised mess on returning from an absence is very frustrating and time-consuming. As a cover supervisor or supply teacher, judgements about your professionalism are made not simply on the quality of your teaching but also on the way in which you manage behaviour, give feedback to the regular teacher and the condition in which you leave the classroom.

If you expect high standards of preparation from colleagues then you have a responsibility to prepare your own cover work with meticulous care. I know that there are emergency situations which dictate that you must pass over the setting of work to others, but these are rare. For each class that you teach you need to have some simple, photocopiable information sheets that give the cover teacher an overview of the students they will be teaching (see Why not try this? on page 184). Include details of the context of the lesson set within the module of work. If your subject is a practical one, then you need to make a decision about whether you will set an active or written task. It is often tempting to leave written work to make the lesson easier for the cover teacher, but you will also need to take into consideration the likely reaction of the students. If students have been working practically and are suddenly confronted by written work, this can often be more difficult for the cover teacher to manage than continuing with the practical. You will find a few colleagues may object to teaching practical and active lessons; do not allow this to affect the quality of the cover work that you set. You cannot allow your expectations to be lowered simply because a colleague is asking for a 'sit down and be quiet' cover lesson. Over the years I have been surprised by the number of colleagues who, although initially cautious, have enjoyed covering practical and active lessons. They gain an insight into your teaching and learning styles and often see students in a different light. Good practice is shared and colleagues who are more used to a traditional and formal classroom begin to see and experience different learning environments. Your students will appreciate the continuity of learning and routines and are better placed to offer help and advice to the cover teacher.

Watch out for ...

- Students trying to leave the room. You may be covering for a teacher who doesn't have the same routines for leaving the teaching space as you do. Make it clear to the students that as this is a cover lesson there will be no opportunity to leave the room (except for urgent toilet visits) without prior written permission. This will preclude students roaming the corridors and advertising to the rest of the school that they have 'got one over' on the cover teacher. →

Watch out for ... continued

● Passing over incidents and not following them up. You have a responsibility to follow up incidents that occur while you are covering lessons. Colleagues will appreciate and recognise your commitment to the students and school if you make it clear that you would like to be as involved as possible in following up incidents or rewards.

● Ignoring other adults in the class. If another adult is present in the classroom, they are there for a reason. Even if their remit is to help one particular student, they will have valuable information about how the class usually runs. Find an opportunity early on in the lesson (if not before it begins) to ask for their advice and involve them fully in the teaching.

● Lessons with students who are much older or younger than you regularly teach. You may need to make adjustments in your physical and verbal language. Raising your voice to a Year 1 class may elicit a different response to that of Year 6 students, and give you unpredictable results. I remember reducing an entire Year 2 class to tears by inadvertently raising my voice above their level of tolerance, after spending three weeks teaching much older children.

Reflecting on practice

Arriving for a day's supply teaching at a Primary school in Newham, East London, I was shown to my classroom by the headteacher. The fact that it was a Portakabin was disappointing but not surprising; however, what I found inside was shocking. There were no displays; random bits of students' work were piled high on most surfaces and resources were scattered everywhere. The headteacher explained that the class had not been taught by a regular teacher since the beginning of the school year (it was then April). I remember thinking at the time 'Okay, but does that excuse the state of the classroom?' I diplomatically bit my lip.

As I cleared a space on the carpet for the class I anticipated a raging horde of feral children running me ragged all day. As they started to arrive I quickly changed my expectation. They were polite, welcoming, eager to learn and followed instructions. I think they were relieved to see an actual teacher in the classroom! Together we set about creating displays, organising the classroom, dusting off the reading scheme, saving and displaying work and making activity areas. Nothing revolutionary, just simple classroom organi-

→

sation and presentation. By the end of the day a classroom stood out from the Portakabin. The headteacher arrived to sign my form and was taken aback. She was amazed and impressed that I had taken the time and effort to improve the learning environment and asked me to stay for the rest of the term. I was only too pleased to accept: the children were lovely and I sensed that they would appreciate the consistency.

Having reflected on this experience and been in the position of engaging supply teachers I am convinced that the expectations of them are simply too low. The headteacher expected very little from me and clearly had expected little from those who had gone before. If schools allow supply staff to turn up on the bell, leave at 3.15 and babysit in between, they are shooting themselves in the foot. Good supply teachers (and there are many) know that it is not enough simply to turn up, supervise chaos and then leave. They also know that the more committed and enthusiastic they are to teaching the class the more chance they have of success. Furthermore, they know how to get repeat work. Good supply teachers accept the same level of responsibility for all aspects of teaching and learning as regular staff, including general housekeeping duties.

If you arrived at your local surgery to find a locum doctor who told you that he wasn't interested in doing any work and he was getting paid at the end of the day anyway, you would probably report him to the General Medical Council. So why accept a parallel lack of professionalism from a supply teacher only interested in her wages?

Cover lesson checklist

- Check procedure for calling on assistance from senior colleagues.
- Check seating plan (if any).
- Check through the register for any names that need practice pronouncing.
- Meet the students at the door with labels.
- After the register, briefly introduce rules, rewards, sanctions structure.
- Apply and model structure by delivering immediate rewards to two or three students.
- Apply and model sanctions structure when appropriate, but preferably as early as possible in the lesson.
- Record (for information only) the rewards and sanctions that you distribute in the lesson.
- Make a point of leaving the room tidy and orderly.

- Feedback positively to the regular teacher.
- Follow up on any incidents and referrals to senior staff.

Why not try this?

Create a photocopiable feedback sheet to use when you cover a lesson for a colleague. Provide a strong model for your expectations of cover work and they may well reciprocate. You might like to consider including:

- An opportunity to give positive feedback on individual students
- Space to record details of students who reach the upper levels of the sanctions list (for information rather than action)
- A tick list for the teacher to quickly and easily give feedback on the work set
- A box to say where the work/resources have been left
- Space for feedback.

There are cover lesson pro formas you can create on the website at www.pearsoned.co.uk/essentialguides.

Key ideas summary

Key idea	Benefit for the teacher	Benefit for the students
Before the lesson read through the cover work and check procedures and routines.	Preparing for the lesson in advance gives you more time in class to focus on the students. When incidents occur you know the correct system of referral and can use it instantly.	There is continuity in teaching and they have confidence in the teacher.
Meet and greet students at the door with enthusiasm for the lesson.	Demonstrates clear commitment to the students and the lesson. Communicates a proactive and assertive approach to the management of behaviour.	Raises expectations about the level of work required in the lesson and discourages negative responses to the absence of their regular teacher.
As a first step explain the rules, rewards and sanctions that will operate in the lesson.	Creates a clear, simple and usable framework for the management of behaviour.	Students are able to predict your responses to appropriate and inappropriate behaviour. They begin to view you as fair and consistent.

Key idea	Benefit for the teacher	Benefit for the students
Model your response to appropriate and inappropriate behaviour by using the rewards and sanctions early in the lesson.	Establishes your control of the class and clearly communicates your expectations.	Students understand that their behaviour has a direct effect on your response.
Leave the room tidy and organised and give some thought to feeding back to the regular teacher.	Colleagues make positive judgements about your professionalism and commitment to teaching their classes.	Students understand that you respect their classroom. The choices they make about their behaviour in the cover lesson have a wider audience.

Strategies for Primary, Secondary, FE and HE

Primary

Start with a gentle game, exercise or reading that you can use to demonstrate to the children how kind/calm/well behaved/intelligent they are. At the moment during this first activity that the class are focused, calm and quiet, persuade them that they are an excellent class who listen attentively and follow instructions fast. Use this moment to refer back to as the lesson develops and some behaviour drifts.

Secondary

Focus your energy on enthusiastic reinforcement of appropriate behaviour from the outset. Over-rewarding students will make you appear insincere. Praise and reward is difficult to accept from someone you don't know well, 'He gave me 10 merits just for sitting down.' Similarly, an over-aggressive and threatening start to the lesson may be disruptive. It will confuse some and tempt others to plot revenge.

FE and HE

If the subject that you are covering is not your own, you may have a class who knows more than you do. Use this to your advantage and ask them to bring you up to speed by teaching you the key aspects of the course/module/scheme. Map the ideas together and ask them to place this lesson in the context of the course. At the same time, highlight aspects of the learning that you can help them develop in this lesson, due to your expertise in complimentary areas.

30 days to make a change

Think about the changes that you would like to make in how you manage cover lessons. This might relate to an individual student, class or context. Commit to the new strategies for 30 days to allow them to embed into practice and your own teaching style.

In 30 days I will walk into work and ....

....

....

....

....

Make a commitment to try some of the strategies that have been suggested in this chapter.

My personal resolutions are:

1 _____   Review date _____

2 _____   Review date _____

3 _____   Review date _____

Managing behaviour around the site

'You and I are now in confrontation, but I see no violence.'

(Steve Biko)

The principle

Your responsibility for managing behaviour does not stop at the classroom door. If you observe students behaving inappropriately in the corridors/lunch queue/school drive/playground you must not ignore it for a quieter life, but address the behaviour. Your work is contributing to the work of the team of teachers seeking to ensure high standards of behaviour throughout school/college life. You are giving something to the communal pot. The proactive approach that you take to managing behaviour around the site can result in a huge improvement in the quality of your working life and the behaviour of students.

The practice

In the classroom the management of behaviour is complex, but at least you control the environment and the audience is limited. In the playground, corridors, dinner hall, car park, gates or street outside, the game is very different. Now, interactions with students happen with a larger and more diverse audience in an environment that you cannot control or predict. Your own behaviour is being scrutinised more intensely and students can feel that you are encroaching on territory where they are used to more privacy and freedom. There are two things that you need to focus on: keeping your physical and verbal language clear and unambiguous, and knowing when to send for help, to record and/or walk away.

In walking around the site you may observe more school rules being broken than you do in the course of your classes. You cannot expect to deal with each misdemeanor personally or immediately and you will need to prioritise those that you do. The reason for this is entirely pragmatic – if you stopped and intervened every time you saw a rule being challenged you might not make it across the site before the end of break. Also, there are those behaviours that need immediate intervention and those that can be recorded for discussion later: 'Hi Adam, thank you for arriving on time to my lesson; when I get time in this lesson I will need a quiet word about some of the poor choices you made in the lunch queue today.'

TOP TIP!

If you are intervening with a student that you don't know or don't usually teach, it is worth finding out their name and form group before you approach them. Casually ask a child who is some distance away from the action for this information and it will be readily given; demand it from the protagonist when you arrive on the scene and it will display your lack of knowledge and put you at an immediate disadvantage.

Walking around the site you can step into difficult situations with students that you don't teach. The ratio of students to teachers can be even higher than it is in your classes and students recognise this; some use it to their advantage. As there are unlikely to be rules displayed in social areas you will need to make the reason for your intervention immediately clear: 'Hello Ryan, I need to have a quiet word with you away from the crowd. I have stopped you because you were swearing/smoking/levitating.' Remember to use a model of the student's previous appropriate behaviour to encourage them to make better choices. If you don't know the students try, 'You don't strike me as the kind of student who would …'. Ask them to consider what actions they are going to take next: 'When we have finished this conversation, tell me what you are going to do/where you are going next.'

Just as you would in the classroom, you need to connect the observed behaviour with the appropriate rule. If your school or college relies on a 'code of conduct' for behaviour around the site, then use this and make a note to appeal to the senior management for an agreement on clear rules for social areas.

Perhaps your greatest contribution to managing behaviour around the school site is your presence. If you have your coffee in the playground, your lunch with the students and are ever-present in the corridor outside your classroom, students will see consistency in your expectations for behaviour both in and out of class. They will grow used to your interventions in social areas and your presence will slowly have an impact on their behaviour. Hide in your classroom or take the long way round to the staffroom to avoid potential problem areas and you risk being effective only within the confines of your teaching space.

The great CCTV and 'security' rip-off

Working with a large FE college on the design of new buildings I was struck by the cost of security: Hawk-eye CCTV cameras, knife arches, security barriers and card scanners, x-ray machines, walls of monitors, offices filled with computer hardware. It promised to bring security, at a price. We knew the promise would be empty. People's behaviour changes not because they are being watched by a camera or stopped by a barrier, but because they are being supervised. We resolved to spend the money elsewhere and to create a positive climate at the entrance rather than one of fear. The idea was simple: to ask the senior and middle managers to stand at the entrances at the beginning of the day and welcome students. Students were met with a smiling face, a kind word and a gentle drawing of the boundary between the college and the outside world. Students responded extremely well, enjoyed the interaction and adjusted their behaviour accordingly. The practice continues to this day and with well-trained site staff providing the same welcome throughout the day the site is safe, secure and free from intruders.

Changing an atmosphere

School and colleges where the corridors and social areas have become almost no-go areas for teachers have found that the staff working en masse can have a direct and immediate impact. One or two teachers patrolling the grounds or monitoring corridors can have little calming effect on the atmosphere; it is just fire-fighting. However, when larger numbers of staff:

- patrol the grounds
- stand outside their classrooms at the change of lessons
- help out at the entrances and exits at the start and end of the day
- sign up to a strategic plan for enforcing no-go areas
- minimise permission for students to be out of classrooms
- rigidly enforce and use 'out of lesson' passes
- swiftly respond to a request to assist a colleague

… there is an immediate change in student behaviour. Of course there needs to be a willingness to confront poor behaviour, but with the staff out in numbers there is less chance of a confrontation exploding and more chance of support arriving if it does. There is obviously an issue with disruption of teachers' allocated breaks, but the outcome is worth the sacrifice and inconvenience. Instead of corridors full of wall climbers, crowd surfers and crisp sprinklers, with collabo-ration between staff they can be calmer; vulnerable students can walk with more confidence.

Showing commitment to the management of behaviour around the site has a number of positive benefits for the individual teacher. Once you have established yourself not simply in the classroom but around the site, the pay-off will be significant and will positively affect each working day. When students realise that you are going to intervene (or record and chase) rather than ignore, they start to correct their behaviour before you arrive or at least smile knowingly and wait until you have passed. Instead of walking into regular and unpleasant negative exchanges with students, you take the opportunity to have positive interactions as you move around the school. Cover lessons are easier, break and after-school duties calmer and more enjoyable. Students are more used to having you around and you are more relaxed in their company. Everybody benefits. You could, of course, spend most of your working day avoiding interaction with children, but then you would be in the wrong job, surely?

Supporting colleagues effectively

Unless you are a senior teacher, you are more likely to come to the aid of a colleague in social areas than in a classroom. When a colleague asks for support, be ready to listen carefully before deciding on your course of action. Judging how you can give the most effective support to a teacher who appears to need assistance but has not asked for it is more difficult. If the situation that you walk into is a confrontation between a student and a teacher (or looks likely to develop into one), consider separating the two and giving everyone time to calm down. 'Could you wait there, Alexandra, I want to speak to Mr Patel in private and then I will have a chance to talk to you', not only buys you time but gives everyone the opportunity to consider their next move. While the other teacher explains the situation, control your verbal and physical reaction to the information. You are being observed carefully by the student involved to see if you are rushing to a judgement. With your face as neutral as possible, listen actively to your colleague and either adjourn the decision-making for later in the day or move the discussion to a less public area. 'Thank you. Yes, we need to deal with this. I will take Alexandra to wait in reception/wait with her form tutor (somewhere neutral and safe, as opposed to outside the Head's office) so that we can organise a better time/place to resolve this.'

If you are supporting a colleague who has lost control of the situation and/or himself or is in the middle of a loud conversation, your 'Mr Patel, can we talk in private?' may need to be more forceful and rhetorical. Another useful way to break into the confrontation is to address the student first, picking up on their immediate behaviour rather than making any judgement on what has gone before: 'Wayne, I know you can be calmer and more polite than this', or, 'Wayne, we need to move this conversation to somewhere more private.' Your comments to the student should serve two purposes: to disengage them from the argument with the other teacher, and to gently suggest to everyone that there would be a better way of resolving the problem.

Fighting in social areas

It is more common for fights to break out in social areas than in lessons: in the lunch hall, on the playground, in the corridors. They are often planned so that there are few teachers in the vicinity and so it is likely that you will arrive while the fight is in progress, or to pick up the pieces. There may be a problem with other students crowding round and in some cases encouraging the fighters. In these cases resist the temptation to rush to an instant judgement on blame but use the strength of your voice to instruct the crowds to leave – 'It's over, finished; we will deal with this now', while treating the fighters equally but separately, 'Kylie, go with Mrs Wallis; Sheena, come with me.' The fallout from a fight can be exacerbated by assumptions of guilt, 'Fighting again, Darren? Right, I'm going to send you home', or by unequal treatment of students, 'Go and clean yourself up Shona; Eleanor, it's the Head's office for you.' Instead, ask witnesses to record their version of events in isolation and take time to reach your judgements on appropriate sanctions or referrals.

Fights at the school gates

Nobody relishes duty at the school gates at the end of the day. In some schools, the gates attract unwelcome visitors: excluded students, dealers, students from rival schools, older teenagers in cars, etc. Teachers are rightly unsure of their jurisdiction on the street outside and managing physical confrontation is more complex and more dangerous. If you are supervising at the school gates you should not do so alone and, to reduce risk further, you ought to have a walkie-talkie to call for more support. If a fight breaks out in the street outside the school, call for more support immediately and ask students who are leaving the site to return to the reception and wait for instructions. If you see weapons being used or produced, call the police; protect those in immediate danger and record what you see. In most of the schools I have worked in where such fights are common-place, the police are already nearby or waiting outside the gates to assist the safe passage of students.

Diverting a confrontation – prevention or diffusion techniques

- Distraction – phone call, urgent message, etc.
- Recognising the early stages of a behaviour sequence and intervening early.
- Leading/inviting the student away to a quieter, less public space.
- Removing the audience.
- Listening/not reacting, waiting for the anger to subside.
- Lowering the voice and softening vocal tones.
- Softening your physical language.

- Repeating a key word or phrase such as 'Keep your hands down'.

- De-personalising the confrontation, 'Try and get control of your anger' rather than, 'Get control of yourself!'

- Offering help rather than criticism, 'What do you need me to do?', 'Do you need to be left alone?', 'Would you like to sit down?', 'Is there someone you need to speak to?'

- Asking questions or suggesting alternatives rather than giving advice or instructions.

Watch out for ...

- Audiences gathering – deal with them as soon as possible: they will inevitably become involved and are never going to improve the situation.

- Judging situations too quickly or too harshly – beware of heightened emotional states and that you may only be seeing a snapshot of the incident at its end.

- Shouting empty threats from a distance and walking away without engaging with the student, 'I can see you, I am going to report you to the Head.'

- Jumping into confrontation too quickly – take your time, control the interaction at your own pace.

Reflecting on practice

Extreme break duty

Break or playground duty is the bugbear of many teachers' day. I would often find myself caught up with dealing with the aftermath of a busy Year 9 lesson only to be harried outside by the PE teacher who was a stickler for 'duties'. It was not that I thought it unimportant, only that those immediate crises inevitably overtake you. Ryan was not going to thank me for leaving him in tears, bag broken, with baying hordes waiting for him, so that I could see to the masses outside. In a school of 1,400 the playground is a very busy place.

That day I had arrived on time. I had thrown caution to the wind in not preparing the room properly for the arrival of Year 11, Set 4 after break (I knew that I would regret it later) and with the voice of the PE teacher ringing in my ears ventured out into the cold. In my previous schools, playground duty had always been a fairly calm affair: dissuading the smokers by patrolling their haunts, dealing with cuts and bruises, the odd fight between two individuals, nothing that I found particularly dangerous or threatening. That day the atmosphere was very different.

Two distinct groups existed in the school and in the community. They learned together in some harmony, considering their turbulent history, but there had been trouble outside school between the adults in the community and now the boys lined up at opposite ends of the yard preparing to settle the score. As I watched they slowly moved towards each other and colleagues ran for assistance. I found myself in the middle of the converging armies and decided to stay put. I adjusted my body language so that I was not threatening anyone and in order not to show preference to either group stood facing away from both, looking down. Now, I am not a small man, but there were individuals bigger than me and regardless of my size there were upwards of 200 students involved. They stopped either side of me and I calmly explained, briefly looking at each lead boy in turn, that it wasn't going to happen here, now, with me in the middle of it. They paused, thought, and with a general murmur of agreement walked away.

The senior management team, watching the whole encounter on security cameras (presumably installed to supplement a physical presence rather than replace it), breathed a heavy sigh of relief, whilst making a mental note to have stern words with me about my personal safety.

Now I am not claiming to have solved the conflict, nor am I suggesting you jump into the middle of gang fights on a whim, but it serves as an example of how simple verbal and physical language can help to calm even the most extreme situations around the school.

Why not try this?

List five behaviours that are a common annoyance as you walk around the school:

1

2

3

4

5

Plot these behaviours on the radar opposite according to the response you will give.

→

Physically intervene – centre circle
Call for support before intervening – inner ring +1
Verbally intervene – inner ring +2
Record and challenge later – outer ring

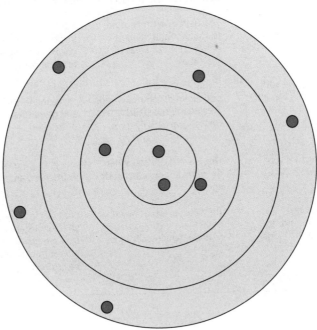

This technique should help you to be consistent and keep a clear perspective on days when your annoyance at a minor infringement threatens to escalate into a confrontation. Now organise and prioritise the following behaviours so that they fall clearly into one category or another:

Damage to school property

Breaking school rules (minor infringements)

Aggressive behaviour

Smoking

Physical bullying

Fighting

Swearing

Racist language

Threats of violence to other students

Threats to staff

Key ideas summary

Key idea	Benefit for the teacher	Benefit for the students
Do not ignore or avoid inappropriate behaviour around the site.	Teachers assert their right to monitor and manage behaviour in all areas of the site.	Students know that their inappropriate behaviour will be challenged and will result in consequences.
Keep your physical and verbal language clear and simple.	Confrontations are discouraged, communication is clear and unassailable. Defensive reactions from students are minimised.	Students recognise the challenge to their behaviour and do not feel personally threatened.
Plan and structure your intervention with care.	The teacher controls when the intervention starts and ends.	Students are given clear instructions and/or choices.
When supporting colleagues, be quick to listen and slow to judge.	The teacher avoids being drawn into a confrontation or undermining colleagues.	Students in a heightened emotional state know that they are going to have the opportunity to speak and be listened to.

Strategies for Primary, Secondary, FE and HE

Primary

Your physical language can escalate the problem. As you make decisions on what you are going to say, consider the messages that you are giving with your body language:

- Personal space is circular, cultural and critical
- Side by side while standing
- Eye level or lower when sitting
- Double the personal space when face to face
- Eye contact brief and gentle
- Slow, casual approach
- Respectful distance
- No pointy fingers!
- Non-verbal cues for drawing students away from their peers

- Model obvious physical respect: waiting to speak and not interrupting, head bowed, confident not aggressive.

Secondary, FE and HE

Preparing to intervene around the site is as important as preparing your response to behaviour in the classroom. There are simple strategies that can change the way the interaction begins, develops and ends:

- Find out the name of the student before you approach
- Consider inviting individuals away from the group to speak privately
- Prepare what you are going to say – beginning, middle and end
- Have an 'outline' ready
- Decide if you want to have the conversation in public or private
- Check your audience as the conversation develops.

How to manage a confrontation and stop it escalating

Discuss choices

Clearly and calmly explain the behaviours which you observed, how they relate to the classroom plan and that the student has made a 'poor choices' so far. Tell the student that you want them to make better choices. You are then focusing on the behaviours and the student is less likely to feel personally attacked.

Don't chase secondary behaviours

Focus on the behaviour you are correcting and do not discuss anything else. If the student tries to divert you, tell them that you understand what they are saying but they still have a consequence/need to make better choices in their behaviour.

Plan your interaction

Make sure that you take a moment to structure what you are going to say and keep to that 'script'. Think carefully about your verbal and non-verbal communication. Enjoy the skill of being able to stay in control of the confrontation.

Don't bring up past misdemeanours

Focus on the single, identifiable behaviour that you have seen. All students start each class with a clean sheet.

Remember that you are the adult

Losing your temper will leave you exposed. Try to see the interaction for what it is – an adult helping a child to learn about behaviour and make better choices.

Get on their level, physically

If they are seated, try kneeling or bending over, rather than standing over them.

Avoid negative comments on cultural styles

Students should be allowed to dress themselves and their hair within the agreed limits of the school's dress code and to move as they please, as long as this does not encroach on the space of others.

Respect students' personal space

Students may feel threatened and become agitated if their personal space is constantly violated. This does not mean, however, that teachers should ignore bad behaviour.

Use friendly gestures, not aggressive ones

Avoid pointing the finger; open hands with upturned palms are less threatening.

Use students' preferred name

Ask each student how he/she would like to be addressed in the classroom and then respect that preference.

Ask questions rather than make accusations

Assume that the student is a responsible person. 'Are you ready to begin?' is less confrontational than 'Put your magazine away. It's time to start class', especially when spoken in a concerned and kind tone.

Deal with the behaviour problem in private

Reprimanding or 'shaming' students in front of their peers causes unnecessary embarrassment. Speaking to them privately respects their dignity and self-esteem.

Listen carefully when students speak

Remain open-minded and objective. Consider the messages of students carefully. Avoid interrupting them or offering unsolicited advice or criticism.

30 days to make a change

Think about the changes that you would like to make in how you manage behaviour around the site. This might relate to an individual student, class or context. Commit to the new strategies for 30 days to allow them to embed into practice and your own teaching style.

In 30 days I will walk into work and ....

....

....

....

....

Make a commitment to try some of the strategies that have been suggested in this chapter.

My personal resolutions are:

1 _____   Review date _____

2 _____   Review date _____

3 _____   Review date _____

Pivotal process for institutional behaviour improvement

Ask — Engage all stakeholders (teachers, assistants, students, parents, site staff, admin staff, governors, community representatives) in a meaningful consultation on behaviour management and improvement through an online questionnaire.

Train — Deliver training that motivates, that addresses hearts, minds and skills, that is focused on consistent practical strategies and the behaviour of adults. Offer training to all adults who come into contact with students. Space the training across the first three terms.

Agree — Agree five positively phrased rules that operate throughout the institution, agree the consequences for inappropriate behaviour and the rewards for appropriate behaviour, and agree behaviours that are expected from staff as well as students.

Plan — Design a consistent plan entitled 'This is how we do it here'. Set expectations high and establish a realistic timescale for change. Send the plan to all stakeholders and announce a start date for implementation.

Act — With everyone committing to the communal effort, set a target of 50 days to eradicate one behaviour. Commit to it, pursue it and prove to everyone that when we stand together we can change the most entrenched behaviours and attitudes.

Display — Display the new agreements throughout the institution; on the walls of every classroom and practical area, at the entrance, in dining halls and corridors, in literature, planners and on the back of ID/swipe cards. 'Staff and students have agreed to ...'

Change — Break the link between student behaviour and teachers' emotion by introducing universal behaviour cues that all staff use. Change the mindset to telling students on rather than telling off. Reinforce the power of modelling appropriate behaviour – 'children see, children do'.

Embed — Refine, drive and tighten agreed practice through additional training and development within the middle management.

Persist — As changes bite things may get worse before they get better and students may challenge the new practice. Be dogged in your persistence and stand firmly together as a staff.

Protect — Replace detention with reparation, place the responsibility on individual teachers to repair trust and follow up every time.

Engage — Engage parents/key adults through regular scheduled contact using old and new technologies. Encourage regular positive phone calls and messages to the home. Invite parents to presentations of new policy and practice. Drip feed positive messages and persuade even the reluctant that the institution is changing for the better.

→

Support	Discreet and flexible support for individual teachers: e-mentoring, online forums, free tips, coaching, behaviour surgeries.
Sustain	Provide in-class coaching tailored to the needs of individual teachers and students. Focus training at the heart of practice, build in-house capacity and 'train the trainers'.
Communicate	Honest, non-judgemental and solution-focused collaboration between staff who are managing challenging groups. Creating a culture where behaviour is discussed as professionally as learning.
Review	Agree a date to review new policy and practice and resist appeals to change in the short term.
Evidence	Collect audio and video evidence of best practice within the institution and use this to train existing staff and induct new colleagues.
Redraft the policy	Create the new policy from successful practice using case studies of practical strategies.

You can get free behaviour-management tips and articles that guide institutional behaviour change at www.pivotaleducation.com.

Afterword

Behaviour in education has never been a bigger nationwide issue. The public debate rages. Influential popularist media feed the demand for information by naming, shaming and attacking vulnerable children and schools. Politicians who couldn't manage the average Year 3 class try to convince everyone that they have the solution. Parents feel under attack as they are blamed for everything that doesn't stick to teachers. While everyone searches for the magic bullet, children listen to the debate and wonder if the adult world has lost control.

The issue is not going to go away on its own and teachers are in a unique position to effect change. There are many teachers who have excellent skills in managing behaviour using strategies that they have tailored for their students. There are strategies that work, people who know how to apply and adapt them and teachers who want to learn. The key issue is not whether we know what works, the issue is training.

Behaviour-management training for teachers is at worst non-existent and at best infrequent. When people outside education hear that training in behaviour management on initial teacher-training courses is such a low priority they are shocked (teachers know this already, to their cost). Managing behaviour is a core teaching skill, yet most teachers are lucky if they have had one INSET day to learn more about it, let alone received continuing training. Whilst the single training day can have a benefit, it is rarely effective as a stand-alone event. At Pivotal we continue to lobby for changes to teacher training to improve the skills of every trainee and to create consistency and excellence on every course.

Teachers need training that they can access throughout their careers; intensive initial training followed by regular opportunities to revisit, rework and remember techniques. We need to include competencies in behaviour management as part of assessing effective teaching, introduce elements in self-reviews, observations, departmental training, sharing good practice on managing behaviour. As ever in education it is partly a question of resources and partly of willingness to take action.

The choice is clear. We can wait for society to re-establish the authority of teachers or we can go and re-establish it ourselves.

Bibliography

Barker, C. (1977) *Theatre Games*, London: Methuen.

Britton, J. (1970) *Language and Learning*, London: Penguin Books.

Canter, L. (1992) *Assertive Discipline*, Santa Monica, CA: Lee Canter and Associates.

DCSF (2002) 'Guidance on the use of restrictive physical interventions for staff working with children and adults', Runcorn: DCSF.

DCSF (2004) *Every Child Matters: Change for Children in Schools*, Runcorn: DCSF.

DCSF (2004) *Safeguarding Children in Education*, Runcorn: DCSF 00272004.

DCSF (2005) *The Report of the Practitioner Group on School Behaviour and Discipline* (The Steer Report) Runcorn: DCSF.

DCSF (2008) *Children looked after in England (including adoption and care leavers) year ending 31 March 2008*, Runcorn: DCSF.

Donnelly, L. (2008) 'One in 11 children may have ADHD.' *The Daily Telegraph*, 20 September 2008.

Furedi, F. and Bristow, J. (2008) *Licensed to Hug*, London: The Cromwell Press.

Gardner, H. (1983) *Frames of Mind*, New York: Basic Books.

Goleman, D. (1995) *Emotional Intelligence*, New York: Bantam Books.

Hoban, R. (2002) *Riddley Walker*, London: Bloomsbury.

Lewicki, R. J. and Edwards, C. T., (December 2003) 'Trust and trust building', in: *Beyond Intractibility*, G. Burgess and H. Burgess (eds), Boulder, Co: Conflict Research Consortium, University of Colorado.

Mahony, T. (2003) *Words Work*, Carmarthen, Wales: Crown House Publishing.

Medina, J. (2008) *Brain Rules: 12 Principles for Surviving and Thriving at Work, Home and School*, Seattle: Pear Press.

Ofsted (2005) *Managing Challenging Behaviour*.

Rogers, B. (1991) *You Know the Fair Rule*, Harlow: Pearson Education.

Sigman, A. (2005) *Remotely Controlled*, London: Vermilion.

Vygotsky, L. (1986, revised edition) *Thought and Language*, Cambridge, MA: MIT Press.

Index

Classroom Gems

Innovative resources, inspiring creativity across the school curriculum

Designed with busy teachers in mind, the Classroom Gems series draws together an extensive selection of practical, tried-and-tested, off-the-shelf ideas, games and activities, guaranteed to transform any lesson or classroom in an instant.

Games and activities for
Primary Modern Foreign Languages
Nicky Leeveque

© 2008 Paperback 336pp
ISBN: 9781405873925

Practical ideas, games and activities for the
Primary Classroom
Paul Barron

© 2008 Paperback 312pp
ISBN: 9781405859455

Games, ideas and activities for
Primary PE
Will Allen

© 2009 Paperback 224pp
ISBN: 9781408220382

Games, ideas and activities for
Learning Outside the Primary Classroom
Paul Barron

© 2009 Paperback 256pp
ISBN: 9781408225608

Games, ideas and activities for
Primary Mathematics
John Dabell

© 2009 Paperback 304pp
ISBN: 9781408223208

Games, ideas and activities for
Primary Humanities
Richard Green

© 2009 Paperback 304pp
ISBN: 9781408228098

Games, ideas and activities for
Primary Music
Donna Minto

© 2009 Paperback 304pp
ISBN: 9781408223260

Games, ideas and activities for
Primary Drama
Michael Theodorou

© 2009 Paperback 304pp
ISBN: 9781408223291

Games, ideas and activities for
Early Years Phonics
Lynn Cousins and Gill Coulson

© 2009 Paperback 304pp
ISBN: 9781408224359

Creative activities for the
Secondary Classroom
Mark Labrow

© 2009 Paperback 256pp
ISBN: 9781408225578

Games, ideas and activities for
Primary Science
John Dabell

© 2010 Paperback 304pp
ISBN: 9781408223239

Games, ideas and activities for
Primary Literacy
Hazel Glynne and Amanda Snowden

© 2010 Paperback 336pp
ISBN: 9781408225516

'Easily navigable, allowing teachers to choose the right activity quickly and easily, these invaluable resources are guaranteed to save time and are a must-have tool to plan, prepare and deliver first-rate lessons'

Longman is an imprint of

PEARSON

The Essential Guides Series

Practical skills for teachers

The Essential Guides series offers a wealth of practical support, inspiration and guidance for NQTs and more experienced teachers ready to implement into their classroom. The books provide practical advice and tips on the core aspects of teaching and everyday classroom issues, such as planning, assessment, behaviour and ICT. The Essential Guides are invaluable resources that will help teachers to successfully navigate the challenges of the profession.

The Essential Guide to
Successful School Trips
John Trant

© 2010 paperback
ISBN 978-1-4082-0447-4

The Essential Guide to
Using ICT Creatively in the Primary Classroom
Steve Woods

© 2010 paperback
ISBN 978-1-4082-2497-7

The Essential Guide to
Secondary Teaching
Susan Davies

© 2010 paperback
ISBN 978-1-4082-2452-6

The Essential Guide to
Classroom Assessment
Paul Dix

© 2010 paperback
ISBN 978-1-4082-3025-1

The Essential Guide to
Understanding Special Educational Needs
Jenny Thompson

© 2010 paperback
ISBN 978-1-4082-2500-4

The Essential Guide to
Shaping Children's Behaviour in the Early Years
Lynn Cousins

© 2010 paperback
ISBN 978-1-4082-2502-8

The Essential Guide to
Teaching 14-19 Diplomas
Lynn Senior

© 2010 paperback
ISBN 978-1-4082-2549-3

Longman
is an imprint of

Practical skills for teachers